EFFECTIVE BRAND

LEADERSHIP

Be Different Stay Different ...Or Perish!

First published in 2016 by Libri Publishing ■ Copyright © Chris Edger and Tony Hughes ■ The right of Chris Edger and Tony Hughes to be identified as the authors of this work has been asserted in accordance with the Copyright, Designs and Patents Act, 1988. ■ ISBN 978 1 909818 78 1 ■ All rights reserved. No part of this publication may be reproduced, stored in any retrieval system or transmitted in any form or by any means, electronic, mechanical, photocopying, recording or otherwise, without the prior written permission of the copyright holder for which application should be addressed in the first instance to the publishers. No liability shall be attached to the author, the copyright holder or the publishers for loss or damage of any nature suffered as a result of reliance on the reproduction of any of the contents of this publication or any errors or omissions in its contents. ■ A CIP catalogue record for this book is available from The British Library ■ Design by Helen Taylor ■ Printed in the UK by Halstan Printing

Libri Publishing, Brunel House, Volunteer Way, Faringdon, Oxfordshire SN7 7YR

Tel: +44 (0)845 873 3837

www.libripublishing.co.uk

EFFECTIVE BRAND

LEADERSHIP

Be Different Stay Different ...Or Perish!

Chris Edger and **Tony Hughes**

Foreword by **Paul Charity**

LIBRI
PUBLISHING

Foreword

Paul Charity

*editor, founder and managing director of
Propel Info, the leading news and information
service for UK pub, restaurant
and foodservice operators*

The publication of this book marks a significant point in the history of branded foodservice in the UK – it has come of age. The provision of food and drink on an out-of-home basis is as old as time itself. The UK's network of coaching inns are testament to the systemised provision of refreshments at key geographical locations as travellers made their slow and weary way around the country. For centuries, every town and city in the UK was well-populated with inns and taverns serving their local populations with a hearty if basic offering of recognisable staples.

It is in the last quarter century, though, that the UK foodservice scene has changed beyond recognition, making a quantum leap in terms of the quantity and quality of branded offers. Now the UK foodservice scene lays claim to world-class credentials, second only to the US in combining the key constituent components of individualisation, quality, value and consistency.

Let's rewind to 1990 to get a flavour of the level of progression within branded foodservice in the UK over the past 25 or so years. Branded operators were few and far between. Luke Johnson and Hugh Osmond were still three years away from investing in PizzaExpress and creating a UK-wide network of restaurants. JD Wetherspoon had a turnover of £7m. Pubs were still required to close at 3pm on a Sunday before being allowed to re-open at 7pm. The branded coffee shop hardly existed and branded quick-service restaurants tended to be US imports – McDonald's arrived in the UK in 1973. Food in pubs existed at a basic level of tired staples – and the term 'gastro-pub' was yet to be invented.

Fast forward and progress has been dizzying. The UK now offers world-class branded formats run by world-class individuals. The UK's leading companies have fast-tracked themselves, assimilating the lessons around systemisation offered by our American cousins, who still lead the world in replicable branded offers, driven, invariably, by the power of franchisable retail content. But talent has flooded the UK scene. Our aforementioned leading companies have moved their skillsets on an upward curve, producing talented individuals who have, in many cases, formed their own companies. US companies opening in the UK have also spawned a generation of executives equipped to start their own foodservice brands. High-quality branded concepts are disruptive within their market places. This opportunity has attracted individuals from the professions, banking, law and accountancy, who have relished the challenge to make their mark – and their fortunes – in the entirely democratic world of foodservice: if you offer tasty, good-value food, consumers will seek you out and fill your tills.

The success of the UK's branded foodservice entrepreneurs can be measured in entirely objective ways. UK consumers make the second highest number of eating and drinking out-of-the-home visits in Europe. UK consumers make 142 visits each per annum, second only to Italy, whose figures are skewed by much bigger breakfast usage (30% of all visits) and average 176 visits each year per capita. The UK foodservice market has the biggest domination by brands of anywhere in Europe. In the UK, visits to brands by consumers rose to 58% of all visits in the year to June 2014, up from 52% cent in 2008. (The next highest country is France with 45% of all visits to branded chains.)

The UK dominates the European list of large companies by turnover with circa 40 companies achieving turnover of £100m or more. No other country, besides the US, is producing so many foodservice brands with the universality to appeal to overseas markets. A non-exhaustive list would include Costa Coffee, Jamie's Italian, Wagamama, Caffè Nero, Pret A Manger and PizzaExpress, with the latter attracting investment from a Chinese private-equity buyer, Hony Capital, intent on expanding the brand across China. Lastly, it's worth noting that last year saw 16 new branded concepts opening in the UK each week – an incredible 800 new branded concepts in a single year. My own estimate is that the UK now has more than 2,000 operators of branded foodservice concepts. Some of these smaller, emerging brands will undoubtedly grow into world-class operations with a world-wide operating footprint.

A particular feature of US foodservice has been its versatility in taking global cuisines and creating its own formulations – before re-exporting them. So aside from the US staples of burger, fried chicken and ribs colonising the globe, we have US reinventions of Italian food and drink, in particular, conquering foreign markets – pizza (Domino's, Pizza Hut) and coffee (Starbucks) being the obvious examples. It was with some pleasure that I dined at Soho House in Chicago this year and noted the company had exported its Dirty Burger, Chicken Shop and Pizza East brands to the US in a classic coals-to-Newcastle exercise. Could UK foodservice firms now go one step further and export our systemised and branded takes on Indian, Chinese, Thai, Japanese, Italian and, indeed, US food around the world? Who would bet against it?

By definition, there's a multitude of approaches to the job of serving food and drink outside of the home. It is worth providing a small flavour of how one individual goes about the job of creating a brand. I offer the example of Alan Yau to illuminate the importance of systemised thinking and application. Few can claim to give brand conceptualisation the depth of thought of this multi-brand entrepreneur. The intense and studied Yau has risen from humble beginnings, as the son of parents running a takeaway in King's Lynn, to become one of the UK's most influential restaurateurs – Wagamama, Hakkasan, Cha Cha Moon, Yauatcha, Sake No Hana and Busaba Eathai are among his branded children. Yau notes, interestingly, that the creation of Wagamama was borne of the confidence provided by a rigorous training in process that he learnt when he worked for McDonald's. "The one thing that McDonald's is able to teach you is systems," he said.

This book, *Effective Brand Leadership*, offers a distillation of the experiences of a multitude of entrepreneurs like Yau, whether they are driving their own start-ups or working within a more corporate environment. It breaks new ground in mapping out the architecture of brand creation and the key crucial stages that follow – brand growth and evolution. It also moves beyond these stages by exploring the existential threats to brand vibrancy and success, and the key steps required to breathe new life into brands that have lost their way.

Its authors, Chris Edger and Tony Hughes, are uniquely placed to provide this articulation of the UK branded foodservice sector's collective reflection on brand creation, development and renewal. They combine intellectual rigour with the hands-on experience of working for many years for Mitchells & Butlers, in many ways the UK's key early day corporate originator of branded food and drinks offers. Chris Edger spent a number of years in an operational role at the company, oversaw its human resources department and has latterly distinguished himself as the UK's leading teacher and author on the subject of multi-site leadership, working as Professor of Multi-Unit Leadership at Birmingham City University. Tony Hughes oversaw Mitchells & Butlers' pub restaurants division for many years, where a generation of sector executives learned the ropes, creating and developing brands. He is often cited as the most influential brand architect of his generation.

One unique feature of the UK's branded foodservice sector is the willingness of individuals and businesses to share their experiences with true generosity of spirit. In a very competitive environment, it would only be natural to guard hard-won learnings. *Effective Brand Leadership* is testament to this aforementioned propensity of individuals to share their insights. It provides a brains trust of best practice, in the form of detailed case studies, from a wide range of the sector's most accomplished entrepreneurs and executives. The brand revival section is proof of my opening remarks about the sector coming of age. We have reached the stage in the sector's history where certain brands have been around long enough to require reinvention and renewal.

The UK's foodservice sector has enjoyed an enormously successful few decades, creating massive numbers of new jobs as UK consumers respond to the quality, value and excitement of eating and drinking away from home. Brands have driven this success by ensuring consumers are offered consistency. That domestic success has created one of the biggest pro rata markets in the world – and now stands every chance of becoming a major export success. *Effective Brand Leadership* is no less than the summation of what the industry has learned so far. It is an invaluable guide for anyone involved in the sector.

Contents

List of Figures

About the Authors

Professor Chris Edger is the author of *Effective Multi-Unit Leadership - Local Leadership in Multi-Site Situations* (described by the *Leadership and Organization Development Journal* as 'one of the key books of its kind for this decade'), *International Multi-Unit Leadership - Developing Local Leaders in International Multi-Site Operations, Professional Area Management - Leading at a Distance in Multi-Unit Enterprises* (two editions), *Franchising - How Both Sides Can Win* (shortlisted for the 2016 CMI Management Book of the Year) and *Area Management - Strategic and Local Models for Growth.* Described by some commentators as the UK's leading expert on 'multi-site retail management', Chris frequently features in the media having appeared on or written for outlets such as Channel 4 News, ITV, BBC News Online, City A.M., Propel Info, the Retail Gazette, the *Daily Mail*, the *Guardian*, the *Telegraph*, *Retail Week*, *Drapers* etc. Previously, Chris had a successful career in the food service and FMCG drinks industry spanning 23 years, incorporating many senior positions in UK and internationally owned organisations. He holds a PhD (ESRC Award) from the Warwick Business School, an MSc (econ) with distinction from the London School of Economics, an MBA from NBS and is a Fellow of the CIPD. He currently teaches at Birmingham City University, Warwick Business School and the University of Birmingham.

Tony Hughes started in the hospitality industry with Stranneylands in 1967. Following a spell as Operations Manager for Duttons Restaurants in the north-west of England, he moved south as Operations Director of Beefeater Steakhouses. Over a 22-year career with Whitbread Plc he had numerous responsibilities; not least acquiring and establishing TGI Friday's in the UK. Tony joined Bass Plc in December 1995 (now Mitchells & Butlers Plc), becoming the board director responsible for developing brands such as Toby, Vintage Inns, Premium County Dinning, Village Pub & Kitchen, Miller & Carter and acquiring Harvester, Browns and Alex in Germany. He is widely credited with transforming Mitchells & Butlers into the country's leading pub and restaurant branded company during his time in post. During his career, he was awarded the Hotel & Caterer 'Catey', voted The Retailers' Retailer 'Best Individual' by the Pub & Restaurant industry in both 2002 and 2006, and received a Lifetime Achievement Award from the European Foodservice Summit in Zurich in 2007. After retiring from Mitchells & Butlers in 2008, Tony served on the board of Rossinter in the former USSR; he still remains on the board of The Restaurant Group Plc in the United Kingdom as their Senior Independent Director.

Acknowledgements

The authors would like to thank (in case-study order) the contributors to this book: Misha Zelman (founder, Burger & Lobster), Jamie Barber (founder, Cabana), Berry Casey (founder, Haché), Andy Laurillard (founder, Giggling Squid), Russel Joffe (founder, Giraffe), Jillian McLean (founder, Drake & Morgan), Andrew Emmerson (ex-Executive Director Development, Domino's Pizza Group), Tom Byng (founder and CEO, Byron), Sue and Paul Salisbury (co-founders of the Premium Country Dining Group), Ian Dunstall (UK brand guru), Vanessa Hall (CEO, YO! Sushi), Patricia Thomas (ex-Executive Director Operations, Domino's Pizza), Frank Steed (ex-CEO of some of US's largest brands), Alan Jackson (former MD, Beefeater Restaurants and Chairman of The Restaurant Group), Karen Forester (CEO, TGI Friday's), Jens Hofma (CEO, Pizza Hut), Kevin Todd (former Director and General Manager, Toby Carvery) and Philip Harrison (founder, Harrison Design).

Both authors would also like to thank Paul Charity, MD and Editor of Propel Info, and Paul Jervis, Managing Editor, Libri Publishing, for their unwavering support throughout the whole process of writing and researching this book.

CHRIS WOULD LIKE TO DEDICATE THIS BOOK TO HIS SON, MAXIM, WHO HAS BEEN A TOWERING SOURCE OF INSPIRATION DURING HIS BACK-TO-BACK AUTHORSHIP OF NUMEROUS BOOKS ADDRESSING LEADERSHIP WITHIN RETAIL SERVICE CHAINS.

TONY WOULD LIKE TO DEDICATE THIS BOOK TO HIS WIFE, GLYNIS, FOR BRINGING LIGHT, LOVE AND LAUGHTER TO HIS LIFE AND TO HIS CHILDREN RICHARD AND KATHRYN FOR GIVING HIM PURPOSE.

'The only sustainable competitive advantage is to learn faster than the competition and to be able to act on what you have learned!'

Jack Welch

Introduction

The UK is experiencing explosive growth in food service concepts. Chain restaurant and food outlet numbers grew by 258% between 2008 and 2015, during which time an estimated 500-plus 'fledgling' food service brands were launched into the UK (Charity 2015a, b). Absolute outlet growth has been impressive – in 1998 there were 4,869 outlets in the UK classified as chain restaurants and food outlets; by 2015 there were 17,450, with total numbers expected to hit over 25,000 by 2020! The reasons for this growth include customer demand for new types of cuisine, premise availability due to the contraction of land-based retail (due to online channel growth), an accelerating trend for eating out or grabbing food on the go and 'operator opportunism' (creating a concept and getting it to scale with the intention of selling it on and cashing in). There is clearly immense momentum in this sector, which is experiencing an unprecedented 'bull run'. However, given the amount of capital being committed to this industry, the question for investors backing this growth is which brands are likely to survive and prosper? What are the criteria for success? And for food service **brand leaders**, how do you get your concept to stand out from the crowd, ensuring you build a successful, sustainable brand rather than waste your money and effort on constructing a 'here today, gone tomorrow' fad?

So what makes a strong, enduring and successful food service brand? The following definitions of service brand key success factors are helpful:

> A strong service company stands for something that is important to targeted customers: the brand not only differs from competitive brands, it also represents a valuable market offer…
>
> (Berry 2000: 132)

> [T]he promise of a bundle of attributes that somebody buys… [T]he attributes that make up a brand may be real or illusory, rational or emotional, tangible or invisible…
>
> (Ambler and Styles 1996: 10)

Useful as these definitions are – stressing differentiation and an idiosyncratic bundle of rational and emotional attributes – they are similar to most generic service branding definitions which focus purely on customers. In contrast, our definition for food service brand success stresses the importance of 'shaping' the brand around both employees and customers:

> Category-leading food service brands are built around a compelling culinary proposition with distinctive functional and emotional benefits that satisfy the needs, feelings and aspirations of both employees and customers, resulting in greater attraction, loyalty and advocacy… (that in turn lead to growing sales, profit and reputation for the owner).

This definition will be further explored later, but our view – based on intensive academic research into service chains and launching some of the UK's most iconic food service brands – is upfront and clear. *First*, brands are conceived and shaped by visionary and dynamic leaders. *Second*, food service leaders build and sustain strong brands (whatever their lifecycle stage) by having a laser-sharp culinary positioning which is constructed to offer uplifting distinctive functional (product and economic) and emotional (psychological and sociological) benefits that create strong bonds with *both employees and customers*, driving positive behaviours and outcomes for the brand. It is this symbiosis which is key. A 'big idea' for a food service brand will exploit a 'space with market place' but ultimately effective brand leaders must ensure that their brand's employees *and* customers simultaneously engage with and drive the brand's growth. And importantly – to reiterate – this is maintained not only through the process of *originating* brands (the focal area for most books on service brands) but also through the processes of *escalation, evolution* and/or *revival* otherwise they will *perish*. It is the definition provided above and the accompanying insights/concepts relating to leader transitions that inform both the overarching model (see Figure 1) *and* the structure of this book which seeks to explain to readers (operators, aspirant entrepreneurs and students) **the essence of effective brand leadership within the food service sector**.

What Are the Distinguishing Features of Food Service?

In order to begin our odyssey of understanding the dynamics behind effective brand leadership and in order to provide context to the rest of the book, we must firstly explore what the key features of food service are. This is important because – compared to FMCG product brands which can be termed 'tangible and visible' – food service brands incorporate many elements which are intangible and invisible, posing specific challenges for brand leaders within this sector. But what are these distinguishing features? Overall we believe that seven idiosyncratic factors stand out as being particularly important:

1. **Intangibility** – many elements of food service cannot be experienced in the same way as branded goods; indeed, the overall food service experience combines a number of environmental and service-based sensory components that will result in customer feelings of satisfaction or disappointment. Companies must therefore spend a lot of time and effort designing sensory 'cues' in order to positively stimulate customer *mood* and *feelings*. But at every juncture, food service leaders must also remember that they are in the business of managing subconscious expectations as well as the experience; to this extent, they must master the art of *subtly* under promising, then over delivering!

2. **Performance** – whilst branded goods are objects, food service can be viewed largely as an emotional performance whereby the brand is articulated and the mood of the customers is enlivened through the actions and demeanour of *enthusiastic* service providers who are selected, trained and geared up not only to 'animate' routine tasks but also to be proactive trouble-shooters in unexpected and unanticipated situations.

3. **Heterogeneity** – food service offers aim for quality and consistency, but inevitably – due to factors such as distance and local context – they are characterised (in contrast to branded goods) by heterogeneity rather than homogeneity. Major factors here include:

    a. *Personnel* – since food service operations are performed by humans, it is virtually impossible to ensure that the exact same level of service is executed by any two people in the same brand

    b. *Time* – the food service offer will (most likely) differ according to session, occasion and seasonality

    c. *Customer* – levels of customer expectations and perceptions will differ according to aspiration, personality and demographic

    d. *Site* – facilities and locations are unlikely to be homogeneous, due to factors such as investment cycles, premise availability and competitive environment.

Of course, successful food service brand leaders will treat this heterogeneity as an opportunity to be exploited through granting autonomy and empowerment to their employees rather than imposing tight constraints!

4. **On-site production** – unlike branded goods where product is generally manufactured elsewhere and then transported into retail premises, the consumer in food service is on-site during the assembly of food and beverages. Their presence allows them to form a 'bundled' perception regarding quality, value and timeliness. The fact that interlocking ordering, production and service processes are observed, felt and immediately judged by customers experiencing 'multiple touch points' places a high degree of pressure on staff at various junctures of the 'chain of service' to get it right or risk instant (or delayed) admonishment. This means that there is a high on-site requirement for quality control which can only be achieved through high levels of training and shift leadership 'modelling'.

5. **Customer involvement** – unlike branded goods, customers have a high level of involvement in food service in two ways. First, they have an active role to play in either helping or derailing staff during delivery; hence the need for clear signalling and information concerning their *expected* role during the order, consumption and payment process. Second, customers experience the brand with other customers within the confines of the same environment. Hence, food service brands – whilst they pay due attention to the way their staff perform and interact – must also consider how customer experiences are enhanced rather than degraded by the presence of other customers. Achieving peaceful and harmonious coexistence amongst customer groups is a key feature of leading food service brands.

6. **Perishability** – food service offers can be viewed as perishable in two ways. First, food service brands cannot (unlike branded goods) be stored away for consumption. Once the doors are open, the food service brand is perishable in the sense that the costs deployed to satisfy customer needs can only be recovered through stimulating demand to 'sweat the asset'. In this sense, operators of food service brands need to be experts in demand forecasting and capacity management so that they do not waste resources (labour and ingredients) that – once deployed – are highly perishable. Second, food service brands are perishable in the sense that – excluding 'grab and go' concepts – ultimately customers depart without tangible

goods but with perishable memories. The degree to which these memories perish immediately or endure is contingent upon how exceptional an 'experience' they've had, whether good or bad – the former being preferable to the latter! Burnishing great experiences onto the consciousness of delighted customers improves frequency and loyalty.

7. **Evaluation** - customers' judgement of food service brands is a complex process, meaning accurate evaluation of their real thoughts, feelings and future actions is difficult to achieve. Essentially, customer perception of a food service brand is mediated by their initial expectations. But what are these initial expectations – how are they shaped? In part, these will be affected by previous usage and/or the food service brand's positioning, promise and reputation. Given the number of 'moving parts' in food service brand delivery, however, locating and remedying deficiencies to ensure customers become raving advocates is problematic. Service is a fundamental attractor or detractor in food service brands, but must be balanced with what is 'going on' with regards to product, environment and price.

What Are the Key Criteria for Strong Food Service Brands?

If the features above create the idiosyncratic context in which food service brand leaders must operate, what are the key characteristics of strong brands in this sector? Before outlining our own views and unpacking the case study insights of the brand leaders that have contributed to the main body of this book, it is worth considering what has been written on or around the subject to date. Essentially, there are two main streams of work that merit consideration: the practitioner and the academic.

1. Practitioner view

There have been a plethora of 'how I did it' books written by (mainly) founder-entrepreneurs explaining their success in setting up successful food service concepts, far too many to list here. We regard three books as being particularly important and relevant to this work, namely: Ray Kroc's seminal *Grinding It Out* (1977) which describes his journey in systemising and growing the fast-food burger chain, McDonald's; Howard Schultz's *Pour Your Heart into It: How Starbucks Built a Company One Cup at a Time* (1998) which outlines his own business philosophy and the way in which he initially grew the coffee house Starbucks; and Meyer's masterful

Setting the Table (2010) in which he tells the story about how he built up a number of successful concept restaurants, accompanying his tale with informative insights into his approach to the building of great hospitality businesses. So what does each have to offer as advice in building strong brands?

The founder of McDonald's believed in consistency and quality, in terms of both operational execution and location choice, as being pivotal to his company's success:

> We agreed that we wanted McDonald's to be more than just a name used by many different people. We wanted to build a restaurant system that would be known for food of consistently high quality and uniform methods of preparation. Our aim, of course was to insure [sic] repeat business based on the system's reputation rather than on a single store or operator. This would require a continuing program of educating and assisting operators and a constant review of their performance [and] our ability to provide techniques of preparation that operators would accept because they were superior to methods they could dream up themselves… [Also, we concluded] that the only practical way for McDonald's to grow as we envisioned would be for us to develop the restaurants ourselves. Being in the restaurant [real estate] development business would mean that we could plan a strong system in which locations could be developed by McDonald's… [making] the right to operate a McDonald's restaurant far more valuable to a potential operator than if we were franchising only a name…
>
> (Kroc 1977: 86–7)

In his book, Schultz places less emphasis on the 'system' and more on people as being the most important variable in the early years of brand growth:

> Our competitive advantage over the big coffee brands turned out to be our people. Supermarket sales are non-verbal and impersonal, with no personal interaction. But in a Starbucks store, you encounter real people who are informed about the coffee, and enthusiastic about the brand… Starbuck's success proves that

a multi-million advertising program isn't a pre-requisite for building a national brand – nor are the deep pockets of a big corporation. You can do it one customer at a time, one market at a time…

(Schultz 1998: 247)

Meyer continues this theme, highlighting his passionate belief that the cornerstone of any successful and enduring food service business lies in delivering 'enlightened hospitality' that makes a profoundly positive effect on customers' feelings:

Hospitality is the foundation of my business philosophy. Virtually nothing else is as important as how one is made to feel in any business transaction. Hospitality exists when you believe the other person is on your side. The converse is just as true. Hospitality is present when something happens for you. It is absent when something happens to you. These two simple predispositions – for and to – express it all…

(Meyer 2010: 11)

2. Academic view

But what factors do academics believe contribute to building strong brands? The first thing to say is that, until relatively recently, most academic research focused upon tangible product and FMCG branding. However, early pioneers of research into services marketing such as Bateson (1985) and de Chernatony and McDonald (1992) pointed out that many of the principles and insights from goods branding did not apply to experientially led service brands that relied on a strong humanistic element to fulfil the service brand promise and bring the personality of the brand to life. The second thing to say is that there are many streams of literature that are pertinent to service branding (such as the voluminous writing on quality – TQM, Deming, Kaizen, EFQM, Six Sigma – and service operations) that provide important insights for students of service branding but are located in a more 'process'-led approach to improvement. For the purposes of this book – in order to give the reader some context on what has been written before on the subject – we select three bodies of enquiry that are particularly appropriate to extending our understanding of building and sustaining strong food service brands:

Service branding

The first body of work that has great relevance to this book lies in the territory of service branding. Although researchers do not base their research in this area solely upon food service, many of their findings and observations have a high degree of relevance and cross-over for the food service sector. What are the main insights in this area in relation to building strong service brands?

a. ***Brand equity drivers*** – the most widely cited article on service branding – Leonard Berry's 'Cultivating Service Brand Equity' (2000) – argues that strong service branding is important in service industries because it increases the customer's trust of the invisible purchase; enables consumers to visualise intangible products; reduces customers' perceived monetary, social or safety risk; and provides owners an opportunity to differentiate in a homogenised market (where most service is indifferently perceived as equal!). Berry argues that, in order to increase service brand power and customer 'mind share', owners need to focus on four drivers:
   - *Dare to be different* – seek continually to 'defy convention' (an advance on Levitt's distinctions between generic, expected and augmented products in 'Marketing Success through Differentiation – of Anything' (1980) where he argues that firms must continually augment their marketing mix in order to maintain competitive advantage)
   - *Determine your own fame* – provide a valuable market offer that focuses upon unserved market needs
   - *Make an emotional connection* – seize customer hearts by sparking feelings of closeness, affection and trust
   - *Internalise the brand* – make sure the brand is clearly defined for, and understood by, service providers; so that they articulate and exemplify your brand (a point extended by de Chernatony in 'A Model for Strategically Building Brands' (2001) in which he argues that staff are the fundamental 'brand builders' within service brand contexts).

b. ***Key success criteria*** – in 'The Criteria for Successful Services Brands' (2003), de Chernatony and Segal-Horn – having interviewed 28 leading-edge service brand consultants –

conclude that strong service brands must have three fundamental properties:

- *Focused position* – ruthless clarity about what the brand stands for in the minds of the consumer (service brand owners should beware of over communication and too much information as there are limitations to consumers' cognitive capacity)
- *Consistency* – consistent brand delivery amongst all stakeholders (employees, customers, suppliers, investors, communities etc.)
- *Values* – unified internal belief systems and shared values that are underpinned by genuine conviction which result in commitment, loyalty and clear brand understanding.

c. **Service excellence** – extending these notions of consistency and values, this body of work examines how to improve service execution within branded service environments. Writing about the 'service profit chain', Heskett and colleagues (1994) stress the importance of the alignment between internally and externally facing service systems, advancing the notion that levels of external service provision will never exceed internal levels (suggesting that companies should pay due attention to investment in people, technology, machinery and concept design if they want to achieve positive behavioural and performance outcomes). For sure, powerful service brands can have a powerful market positioning and effective customer communications programme but be constantly undermined by poor staff delivery (caused by high levels of turnover, poor morale etc.). What are the solutions?

- *Enlightened HRM* – in order to improve 'internal coherence' within the brand, firms should 'devote as much time to staff as customers' (de Chernatony 2001) through designing appropriate 'brand specific' recruitment, selection, development and reward systems. In addition, staff should be given the resources to do the job, feel involved in day-to-day decision-making and have the autonomy and empowerment to rectify customer issues 'on the spot' (which will lead to the so-called 'recovery paradox' – the phenomenon of great service recovery actually increasing customer satisfaction and loyalty). In assessing the fundamental requirements of motivating and engaging Generation Y and Millennials – who have a completely different value set and world view to those of previous generations – Pink (2011) suggests that firms should focus their employee branding upon key areas of 'mastery, purpose and autonomy'.

- *Invest in moments of truth* – two of McKinsey's most widely read papers – 'The "Moment of Truth" in Customer Service' (2006) and 'Maintaining the Customer Experience' (2008) – make the argument that service firms rarely review what customers really want (properly discriminating between what they say and what they do and feel). Service firms should scientifically evaluate where the true 'breakpoints', 'sensitivities' and 'patience thresholds' lie within their service delivery systems to determine where high and low perceived value lies. Companies should eliminate cost and effort in servicing non-value-added elements of the service chain and focus investment in areas of high perceived customer value. Also, isolating emotionally charged moments of truth which might affect the repeat purchase intentions of customers is vital, with emotions most commonly running high during 'problem events'. Finding a solution to a problem is a key moment of truth for companies; those that provide instant solutions will increase their emotional bonds with their customers and achieve a fair degree of differentiation. Staff are the key lever here, with McKinsey suggesting that service companies commit resources to hiring emotionally intelligent staff, creating real meaning (that addresses thoughts, feelings, values, beliefs and emotional needs), training to improve capabilities and mindsets, proper reward and resourcing structures/processes and exemplar modelling from front-line leaders (who in particular serve as role models for emotionally intelligent behaviour).
- *Customer experience* – in the same vein, articles and books focusing on enhancing the customer experience stress the importance of getting customer perceptions to exceed their initial (or pre-formed) expectations in order to

generate loyalty and even raving advocacy. Reichheld's argument in his seminal article the 'The One Number You Need to Grow' (2003) stresses the need for companies to focus their efforts upon increasing 'strong advocates' who will readily 'recommend the brand to friends and family' to 'drown out' tepid supporters or detractors. But how should they achieve this? In his *The Ten Principles Behind Great Customer Experiences* (2013; winner of the prestigious 2014 CMI Book of the Year), Wilkinson argues that great customer experiences should be designed to reflect the customer's identity; satisfy higher objectives; leave nothing to chance; more than meet expectations; be effortless, stress free, socially engaging and indulge the senses; put the customer in control and always consider emotions.

d. *New world model of branding* – with the rise of digital and social media over the past ten years, commentators have tracked the way in which service brands have adopted a multi-channel approach to reach consumers in order to gain competitive advantage. Their conclusions make sober reading for brand builders (see Edger 2012, 2013, 2014, 2015 and 2016; Edger and Emmerson, 2015). Digital has either accelerated or strengthened consumer trends, which include:
   - *Immediacy* (a need for instant rather than deferred gratification)
   - *Impatience* (increased intolerance for waiting or queuing)
   - *Promiscuity* (greater 'switching' behaviours caused by access to digital real-time comparative data and willingness to trial, moving up or down the 'brand hierarchy')
   - *Sovereignty* (enhanced perceived customer power due to more information and the ability to make 'spontaneous' public, online comments about service performance which – if negative – can discourage a huge number of potential trialists).

This has meant that service brands have had to adapt their philosophies and systems in order to adjust to the new customer paradigm. In his bestselling book, How Brands Grow: What Marketers Don't Know (2010), Sharp contrasts the 'past world view' of brand builders with the 'new world view'. Overturning the received orthodoxies, he suggests that brand builders should (amongst other things) concentrate on: salience rather than positioning; distinctiveness rather than differentiation; 'loyal switchers' rather than 'brand loyals'; granting price promotions for existing customers rather than aiming them at new customers; and competing with all brands in the category rather than just competing on positioning. The overall message of this excellent book is clear – the iron laws that governed the process of growing brands in the past have ceased to be relevant in today's digital age.

Food service brands

Much of the literature on growing strong food service brands echoes many of the points made above by practitioners who described 'how' they created strong food service brands and academics commentating upon the means by which service brands 'set themselves up' for sustainability and prosperity. Amongst the (thin) amount of scholarly enquiry in the food service branding area, three contributions from leading academics merit citation here:

a. **Focal areas** – in his article 'Endorsed Branding' (1998), Chris Muller – the US's leading academic on multi-site food service – makes the point that great food service brands transcend the products and services they offer by positioning themselves through 'secondary meaning' which becomes embedded within consumer minds and becomes extremely difficult to displace by competitors (e.g. KFC's Colonel Sanders' 'special recipe' that makes its chicken 'finger lickin' good'). But – just as importantly – Muller believes that food service brands will only grow in strength and value (simultaneously generating loyalty whilst commanding a price premium) if they relentlessly focus on three key issues:
    - *Quality* – 'best-in-class' products and services
    - *Execution* – seamless service delivery
    - *Image* – establishing a symbolic and evocative 'mindshare'.
b. **Customer perceptions** – Peter Jones, one of the leading food service academics in the UK, and his team conducted an experiment which they reported upon in the article 'Customer

Perceptions of Services Brands: A Case Study of the Three Major Fast Food Retailers in the UK' (2002). Taking de Chernatony's three criteria for successful service brands (focused position, consistency and values), Jones conducted focus groups to establish perceptions of their achievement/fulfilment in McDonald's, Burger King and KFC. His findings were as follows:

- *Focused position* – all three food service companies had a focused position in the minds of consumers (value fast food).
- *Consistency* – there was a variation between perceptions of quality of product and service. Product quality was perceived to be more consistent than service (i.e. machines and food production processes were less susceptible to 'breakdowns' than front-line order taking, service provision and problem resolution).
- *Values* – these were interpreted in two ways. All brands were perceived to provide 'value for money' meals. However, McDonald's was adjudged more values driven with regards to involvement in local community activities.

c. **Public house branding** – the history of food service in the UK is different to that in the US. The 'tied house' pub has – until relatively recently – dominated the food and beverage sector. Home grown and imported food service concepts (particularly fast food and fast casual) have completely transformed the eating 'out of home' landscape but over 55,000 'licensed premises' pubs remain. A proportion of these outlets have been converted into branded chains, but questions remain relating to their viability and sustainability. How do the pub chains successfully grow brands within their estates? For sure, the industry is littered with branded failures. Which brands will succeed and which ones will fail – and why? Early scholarly enquiry into this area by Lincoln and Elwood (1995) argued that 'hard' pub branding would succeed if customers 'perceived the pub concept as a brand' (meeting real needs and expectations). Failing this, they believed it was advisable to pursue a 'soft' branding approach where outlets were badged as a 'loose confederation' for operational focus, control and economies of scale purposes (increasing levels of consistency and quality). Further analysis has suggested that a strong relationship in pub branding exists between clear positioning, *unit scale*, location (physical and demographic) and total brand equity; problematic when many units in this sector have 'legacy' tertiary locations and sub-scale dimensions (Edger 2014).

Brand Lifecycle and Leadership Transitions

The final literature that is most relevant to this book concerns the subject of brand lifecycles and leadership style 'fit' during the various 'transition stages':

a. *Service brand lifecycles* – according to Sasser and colleagues (1978), service firms follow a typical S curve of life, transitioning through the stages of introduction, multi-site rationalisation, growth, maturity and decline. During introduction, firms introduce an innovative new concept with modest sales which they roll out in multi-site formats, rationalising the estate once they have proof tested its positioning and 'locational fit'. Having established a successful model, brands then drive profitable multi-site growth through rapid roll-out, facing limited competition at this stage as their concept has not been copied or understood by competitors to any great extent. However, maturity follows as the competition catches up and sales level off, leading many firms to drop into the decline stage, where sales and profitability drop to levels that threaten their viability. However, as other commentators have noted, there is a high degree of determinism surrounding the firm life-cycle model (Jones 1999; Lechner and Kreutzer 2010). Not all firms respond according to their life stage positioning. In maturity, firms have a range of choices that management can take and some food service brands have been successful (whilst maintaining the 'true north' of the brand) in repositioning their product and service offers. But which leadership style melds with which lifecycle stage?

b. *Lifecycle-leadership style 'fit'* – according to the lifecycle-leadership style 'fit' concept, leadership style requirements differ during start-up, rationalisation, accelerated roll-out and maturity stages (Reynolds et al. 2007). Indeed, Muller (2013) observes that 'as an organization grows, leaders at each stage become "Support

Columns" for the enterprise' but that different leader typologies are required at different stages (entrepreneur during creation/gestation, implementer during construction/survival, navigator during development/growth, harvester during cultivation /maturity and explorer during renewal/legacy). But how adaptive can leaders be to changing requirements – given that personality, traits and capabilities can be somewhat difficult to change at this level? For sure, leaders are sometimes capable of 'growing' with the brand, but often – most frequently following concept development and initial roll-out – visionary pioneer leaders require replacement by rational professional managers who have the tacit skills to leverage brand scale efficiencies. Then problems occur when this 'professional/administrative' cadre is faced with major discontinuities that threaten the enterprise's business model. Their default style of standardised compliance and control leadership is insufficiently flexible to deal with fast changing external environments as they are locked into outmoded thought patterns that are suited to old, rather than new, paradigms. They lack the imagination, ingenuity and tacit expertise to reposition their organisations to a place that is easily understood and accepted by internal and external stakeholders. At this point, a change in leaders is required again – as it was for so many UK service companies during the Great Recession:

> A raft of bosses, from retail to finance and leisure to travel have found themselves heading for the exit as the going gets tough… when times are tough firms have to focus on driving their core business hard – cutting costs and finding *innovative* [author's italics] ways to win market share… Instead of throwing up the flak of a transformational M&A deal to mask more deep-seated problems, cost cutting has become the mantra of the boardroom…
>
> (Steiner 2011: 73)

The point is, however, that different leadership styles and competencies are required for different stages in a service firm's lifecycle. Often that will involve changing the 'captain' rather than expecting him/her to have either the willingness or capability to adapt.

Guiding Model and Book Framework

The central purpose of this book is to establish how effective brand leaders build and then sustain great food service brands. It is a pertinent question within the current climate due to the explosion of concepts launching themselves the into food service marketplace. Some will succeed, but most will eventually fail. Why? Thus far in this book, we have considered the generic features of service brands and commentary from both practitioners and academics on the fundamental building blocks of strong service brands. But what is our position? We agree that food service brands do transition through various life-cycle changes; this knowledge is derived from the fact that we have both written about, researched and run some of the UK's food service brands! Indeed, we believe that there are four distinct **transitions** that brand leaders need to master in order to be successful in their endeavours to *build brand strength*: namely, ***originate, escalate, evolve*** and/or ***revive***. Failure to achieve mastery in these key stages will undoubtedly lead to a parlous state that nobody wants: namely, they will ***perish***. Additionally, however, we believe that there are **universal guiding principles** that either make or break a food service brand, whatever stage the brand is transitioning through. These are summarised both in the definition below and the model in Figure 1:

> Category-leading food service brands are built around a compelling
> culinary proposition with distinctive functional and emotional
> benefits that satisfy the needs, feelings and aspirations of both
> employees and customers, resulting in greater attraction, loyalty and
> advocacy… (that in turn lead to growing sales, profit and
> reputation for the owner).

But what does the definition and its accompanying model – set out opposite – mean and why is each component so important?

- ◘ **'Leader transitions'** – at various points during the lifecycle of a food service brand, different leadership typologies and approaches are exhibited/required, namely: originate ('originator'), escalate ('escalator'), evolve ('evolver'), revive ('reviver') and perish ('pariah'). With the exception of 'pariahs', they attempt to apply our universal principles/characteristics of strong and sustainable food service brands:
  - **'Category-leading food service brands'** – strong, sustainable brands which are category leaders within their niche segment of the food service market.

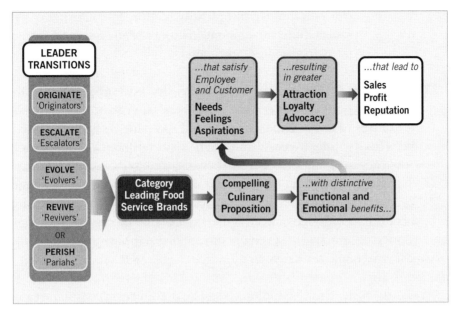

Figure 1 **Effective Brand Leadership Model**

- **'Compelling culinary proposition'** – category-leading brands have an alluring and compelling culinary proposition which is easily understood and welcomed by all internal and external stakeholders.
- **'Distinctive functional and emotional benefits that satisfy the needs, feelings and aspirations of both employees and customers'** – the culinary proposition will be appealing and stand out from the crowd – satisfying basic and higher needs, feelings and aspirations for *both* employees and customers – if it is underpinned by *symbiotic* functional and emotional benefits:
  - *Functional benefits* – these are largely tangible. They are an expression of what the brand offers, designed to meet the *basic economic and product-based* needs of both employees and customers, namely: employees (fair pay, conditions and job security) and customers (assured quality, consistency and high perceived value).
  - *Emotional benefits* – these are largely intangible. They are aimed at addressing higher order *psychological and sociological feelings or aspirations* amongst both employees and customers, namely: engaging culture with tangible recognition, development, values and teamship

(for employees); and identity reinforcement, experiential satisfaction, attachment/in-group affiliation and social participation (for customers).

◘ **'Resulting in greater attraction, loyalty and advocacy'** – this applies to both employees and customers, namely: talent attraction, low levels of turnover/absenteeism and spontaneous 'ambassadorial' behaviours (employees); and high visit frequency and 'raving' advocacy to family, friends and work colleagues (customers).

◘ **'Leading to growing sales, profit and reputation'** – the outcome of a well-constructed food service proposition that offers compelling benefits to employees and customers is financial success (and perhaps a price premium) – if several potential miss-steps are avoided by the effective brand leader along the way!

As stated, we believe this definition should be the 'universal lodestar' of any successful food service brand. The reality is, however, food service brands do not follow a straight line trajectory of success. Their journeys can be convoluted and complicated. Brands can be created and fail immediately: 20% of hospitality businesses in the UK are declared insolvent within the first year and only 40% make it beyond year three. Also, brands can be **originated**, become **scaled** up successfully but then fail to **evolve** and adapt to changing customer requirements – their functional and emotional benefits having become indistinct and boring to both employees and customers alike. Or brands are launched successfully, evolve well but are then undone by managerial complacency or inattention. At this point they either face the prospect of **perishing** or its brand leadership can **revive** the brand – rejuvenating momentum by reigniting its mojo.

But at every lifecycle stage the brand requires a *specific* leadership approach to drive it on. **What are the main dimensions and tasks of effective brand leaders throughout these lifecycle transitions?** Our attempt to answer this question informs the structure and chapter order of this book, in which we analyse qualifiers and differentiators for effective brand leadership through the different phases, combined with significant case-study contributions from some of the industry's most outstanding brand leaders:

◘ **Chapter 2: Originate** – this chapter examines three key areas for effective food service brand leaders during the creation stage, namely:

finding a '*gap*', constructing a *compelling concept* and forming a *vibrant culture* – arguing that brand leaders need to put all three of these key building blocks in order to gain market traction.

- **Chapter 3: Escalate** – this chapter will examine how brands are successfully driven to achieve scale and pre-eminence, arguing that effective brand leaders need to focus upon accelerating their brand *network* whilst simultaneously *systemising* their organisation and driving consumer *awareness*.

- **Chapter 4: Evolve** – having created and rolled out a successful brand built upon solid foundations, effective brand leaders – whilst preserving the brand's core identity and purpose – must ensure it adapts to changing customer requirements to remain 'on-trend'. Hence brand leaders – at this stage of the brand's lifecycle – need to focus on *customer insight* (constantly evaluating how they can better serve their needs, feelings and aspirations) whilst maintaining the ability to land changes quickly through a high degree of *organisational agility* and *implementation capability*.

- **Chapter 5: Perish** – often, however, (formerly) successful food service brands run out of energy and customers. This chapter considers why brands typically bite the dust, examining three major causes which we label a 'trinity of despair' – *managerial incompetence, resource starvation* and/or *product obsolescence*.

- **Chapter 6: Revive** – ailing brands can be recovered and restored back to rude health if they are caught in time by focused, energetic and passionate brand leaders. This chapter outlines how they generally achieve revival through *galvanising the organisation*, whilst simultaneously *sharpening up execution* and *refreshing the brand position*.

- **Chapter 7: Conclusion** – throughout the book, we will have outlined what constitutes effective brand leadership throughout the different lifecycle stages by way of our own observations and the case study contributions of a number of industry leaders. In this chapter we bring all the threads and strands together, distilling out the core essence of effective brand leadership: a mission to '**be different**' and '**stay different**' by crafting and maintaining – what we and our case study contributors term – **distinctive uplifting experiences** for *both* staff and customers. Our 'final, final thoughts' summary highlights what we regard as **four fundamental characteristics** of effective brand leaders across *every* brand lifecycle transition.

As we have said, the case studies in the book (provided by luminaries of the industry) will support all the main sections within the book in order to provide some practical, contemporaneous insights into effective brand leadership. Insights from these case studies will be triangulated in the Conclusion of this book. Our first case study, below, however, is intended to bring to life our overarching definition and framework (see Figure 1) for effective brand leadership within the food service sector.

CASE STUDY 1 – **NANDO'S: BUILDING BRAND STRENGTH**
Chris Edger

In the UK, Nando's has been the stellar performer in the fast casual dining segment of the food service market. But what are the origins of its successful growth and how has it maintained its momentum through successive lifecycle transitions (originate, escalate and evolve) in recent times?

In 1987, Fernando Duarte and Robbie Brozin bought a humble Portuguese eatery in the heart of Rosettenville, South Africa having been bowled over by its mouth-watering PERi-PERi marinated and basted chicken dishes. Over the course of time they rolled and refined a concept which they renamed Nando's. In the UK today, it is a **category leader** in the fast casual dining segment with over 400 stores; attracting a high market share of the 18-to-34 demographic, having grown through word of mouth recommendations rather than national advertising or discount vouchering (something that their competitors have been highly reliant upon). Why has it sustained its momentum through its growth lifecycle?

First, it has a clear and **compelling culinary proposition**: spicy chicken with attitude. Its hero dish consists of *fresh* chicken which is marinated over-night in its *special* PERi-PERi sauce (which has a strong Afro-Portuguese *provenance*, traced back to the African bird's eye chilli) and is then buttered and *fly grilled* on an open flame. Second, its core culinary proposition is buttressed by **distinctive functional and emotional benefits** that flow from the brand to benefit employees *and* customers:

Employee benefits – aside from the fact that it provides market-leading levels of pay and benefits, it has an inclusive, meritocratic people philosophy which is exemplified by this statement:

Nando's is not just about the chicken. It's never been about the chicken. It's about the people who make the chicken... inspired by our adventurous spirit and values of pride, passion, courage, integrity and family...

Nando's is renowned within the sector for valuing its employees highly, strongly believing that treating them well will translate into exemplary customer service behaviours. The company's sense of fun extends to changing the names of some positions (e.g. HR Director to Mother Hen, Transport Manager to Poultry in Motion). How authentic is this approach and to what degree do these 'benefits' turn into positive behaviours? In its citation for being the Best Large Company to work for in the UK in 2014, the company was recognised for outstanding engagement scores, low levels of staff turnover (relative to the rest of the sector), innovative development/progression programmes and industry-leading customer satisfaction scores. Clearly, the 'Nando's way' really resonates with employees, who reciprocate the care they receive from the company by caring about their customers.

Customer benefits – research has demonstrated that the brand delivers strongly to its core demographic both **functionally** – customers believe Nando's fulfils their **need** for 'taste, quality, volume of food and speed of service' – and **emotionally** – customers **feel** Nando's provides 'warmth, a social extension, stress relief, guilt-removing properties, friendly staff and good company'. In addition, the tailored design of each store, high level of 'customer release/involvement' during the 'casual-style' chain of service and vivid sensory cues (sight: fiery orange/red colours; smell: 'spices'; sound: 'busy Portuguese town'; touch: sticky fingers; and taste: 'spices dancing on your tongue') make a visit to Nando's a memorable experience.

Outcomes – the net output of this careful and patient construction of a category-leading food service brand with a compelling culinary positioning which provides distinctive benefits, satisfying Nando's employees and customer's needs, feelings and aspirations has certainly resulted in high levels of attraction, loyalty and advocacy! One of the main outcomes is that Nando's fulfils one of the main criterion of strong brands: namely, the ability to charge a price premium coupled with a 'tight operational model' (due to the casual 'self-serve' nature of the service cycle)... a combination that should ensure Nando's sustains its pre-eminent position within its category for some time to come.

CHAPTER 2   **Originate**

TWO

What are the origins of successful food service brands and how can they achieve originality? Often, their roots can be traced back to passionate zealots - creative Originators who have had a spark of an idea and possessed the spirit and the energy to co-opt others to help them bring their original vision to life. Sometimes their inspiration and desire has been shaped/formed by previous failure or misfortune! Unlike Retail and FMCG (which both have a high levels of industry concentration), Originators in the food service industry *usually* reside in the independent sector, outside large chain environments, where they have the autonomy to express themselves and can focus upon their end goal of landing their concept without interference or red tape. In some instances, Originators are given licence to inhabit corporate domains, usually with the protection and patronage of far-sighted key decision makers (such as the CEO or Chief Marketing Officer). The important point is that Originators require environments with minimal structure and surveillance so that they can move fast to meld their original idea, adapting it successfully to exploit a white space in the prevailing market. Nevertheless, many successful Originators - either consciously or inadvertently - do follow some form of process in order to get their idea off the ground (not least because they will often need to present a business case to potential investors). For instance, Danny Meyer seeks to answer nine 'yes criteria' for new ventures when he is launching a new food service concept:

Meyer's Nine 'Yes' Criteria

1. 'Fit' – the opportunity fits and enhances our company's goals and objectives
2. 'Inspiring' – we have a chance to create a ground breaking, trail-blazing and fresh business
3. 'Timing' – we have the capacity to 'grow with excellence'; we have the capability and talent
4. 'Category Leaders' – we can be category leaders in the niche we are pursuing

5. 'Core Benefit' – our core business will benefit as a result of us pursuing this project
6. 'Passion' – we feel excited and passionate about it; we will learn, grow and have fun
7. 'Community' – we are excited about doing business in this community
8. 'Context' – the context is the right fit and the location is in harmony with our business style
9. 'Safe Investment' – an in-depth analysis convinces us it is a wise and safe investment

(Adapted from Meyer 2010: 273)

But what do we believe to be the essential building blocks for strong brands at an early stage of development?

CASE STUDY 2 – **ORIGINATING BRANDS**
Tony Hughes

Tony Hughes (co-author of this book) has founded and developed a number of category-leading food service brands both in the UK and abroad.

There are three essential components relating to creating a category-leading brand: 'finding a gap' (locating a market space where existing operators perform badly or nobody has 'been' before); 'creating a compelling concept' (exploiting this space with a proposition that 'animates' consumers); and underpinning the entire enterprise with a 'vibrant culture' (something 'inimitable' that competitors can never copy). These three essential cornerstones are dealt with in this chapter, below; in this case study, I want to highlight three key insights that I have observed, learnt and applied over the years during the process of creating successful brands:

◻ **Passion NOT profit motive** – in this chapter, we start off by talking about 'researching the gap' as a precursor to launching a brand… in order for it to set off in the right direction and be financially successful; and, indeed, this is absolutely necessary… However, I believe it to be a universal truth that Originators who invent successful brands ***don't*** start with an underlying profit motive or indeed a 'planned exit'... what they start with is a PASSION... a visceral mission to *make their mark*! Indeed this is one of the main reasons why large companies fail to in their attempts to create great brands; they are generally started with the wrong 'end' in mind – that of profit – rather than a genuine passion for creating something famous and memorable that will stand the test of time! ... successful brand Originators intuitively understand that profit is the 'byproduct of innovation'... that 'creativity is the *leading* edge, profit the *trailing* edge'! ...

◘ **Idiosyncratic brand icons** – we also talk of creating a 'compelling culinary concept' in this chapter... One thing that stands out about successful food service brands is some of their idiosyncratic features; that is to say, they have a number of key iconic 'artefacts or customs' that mark them out from the crowd... Indeed, I would go as far as to say that truly great brands have at least three 'signature' icons that enable customers to immediately identify the brand and – because they are 'fun things that we like!' and seem irrational, fail the 'cost efficiency' test and lack functionality – they bolster the brand's 'non-corporate credentials! ... These icons can be expressed in design, culinary or service delivery terms... the fact is they 'distinguish' the brand from its competitive set, enduring throughout any changes that might occur in later years...

◘ **'First three feet' and 'bookending'** – great food service brands are not only conceived through a passionate mission and *defined* by iconography, they are also *distinguished* by a 'vibrant culture' (see below)... but what should this culture actually aspire to achieve day-in-day out? ... Memorable customer experiences that are delivered in what I call the 'first three feet' and 'bookends' of the brand... A brand can have the greatest design and product but it will come to nothing unless customers experience outstanding service at the 'point of impact'... this first three feet is the moment of truth for any food service brand... the personality of the brand is defined not only by its functional aspects but also its emotional appeal, which is delivered – in large part – by happy, proactive and responsive front-line service providers... What ensures that companies excel in the first three feet? Simple – in hospitality, people *are* the brand in cultures which are built around internal and external customer excellence;

a real desire to identify and satisfy differing customer needs, feelings and aspirations in the first three feet throughout the whole chain of service! ... BUT especially during the first impressions and the last impressions; *bookending* the experience... ensuring that three different people say 'hello!' or 'welcome!' and on departure three different people say 'thank you!' or 'see you soon'... bookending – three 'hellos' and three 'goodbyes'... as the old adage goes, 'you never get a second chance to make a first impression and last impressions last for an awfully long time!'. This is particularly the case in hospitality where patrons often depart with little other than memories...

2.1 Research Gap

The start point for any successful food service brand is a hunch! Either Originators have a gem of an idea which they believe will 'find a place with market space' or they opportunistically stumble across a formula which they believe can become scalable. Most books on brand building tend to give rational explanations for the genesis of brands but the reality is that the origins of most food service brands spring from ad hoc inspiration. However, all successful brands do have one thing in common – they provide a distinctive solution to a customer problem. That is to say, they satisfy unfulfilled needs, feelings and aspirations. At this stage of the process, it is essential that brand builders/founders rigorously research the market to 'sense test' their hunch. But what are the main qualifiers (i.e. hygiene factors) and differentiators (i.e. things that set brand builders apart) in this exercise?

Research Qualifiers

Essentially, Originators need to transition their seed idea into a distinctive and desirable consumer proposition that will assume category leadership. This cannot be effected without some degree of qualitative and/or quantitative research:

- **Identify target customers** – taking the seed idea, Originators should ask themselves: Who would this product serve? What would be its core market? How big is this customer segment? Does it have a growing or shrinking demographic?
- **Understand behaviour** – having identified a viable customer

segment that the 'hunch idea' might address, it is vital that the (changing) needs and aspirations of this cohort are well understood. This can be achieved by focusing on 'ideal' customer types, examining their attitudes and behaviours, asking: What do they value? Where and how do they spend their leisure time? What corollary brands do they use? Why do they use them?

- **Examine culinary tastes and trends** – in addition to understanding behavioural patterns, Originators need to understand where the taste profile of their potential target customer base is migrating towards. In developed markets, customer palates are becoming more discriminating and sophisticated. What types of cuisine are the target customers for this seed idea experimenting with or 'moving into' at present? In addition, preferences for service delivery systems are evolving (most noticeably towards so-called 'fast casual'). How can the Originator exploit this trend for greater access and immediacy? Originators must be absolutely certain that their idea is 'on trend': relevant to prevailing customer needs, aspirations and desires.

- **Evaluate competitive set** – having started with customer research, Originators must now look at their potential competitive set. Those backed with large resources (i.e. those in multi-brand corporates) will be able to 'map the market'. Those with scarce resources must conduct forensic mystery customer visits to likely competitors (during peak and non-peak sessions), asking: How does the competition currently address target customer needs? What do they do well/badly? What are the reasons for their success/failure? How could they be improved? What gaps can we exploit in order to gain immediate competitive advantage?

Research Differentiators

But what sets successful Originators apart from the rest during the initial research exercise?

- **Macro trend 'location'** – those researching 'where the market' is going would be well advised to look outside their own domestic confines to markets further up the 'progression curve' for insights into where customer/competitor behaviour might be heading (for instance, the US 'fast casual' and 'better burger' revolutions have been mimicked in the UK).

- **Micro trend 'location'** – as stated, often companies and individuals looking to develop new food service concepts take a 'macro' view of the current market. Whilst useful in 'sizing clear and present prizes', it carries the danger of giving a 'rear-view' picture. Trend analysis (as stated above) is absolutely essential in giving brand builders essential information on what customer needs and aspirations are gravitating towards. However, Originators would be advised to really drill down deep to understand niche micro-trends: these are where the future market lies. Catching a customer/market 'movement' in its early stages is one vehicle through which brand builders can eventually achieve momentum and ascendancy.

- **Creative plagiarism** – successful brand building is not only derived from invention; it can also be generated from improvement. Some successful food service brands are merely 'plagiarised re-casts', a confection of ideas and inspirations stolen from a range of existing formats and brands. Many food service brands in the UK – for instance – are indebted to their US cousins for ideas and inspiration.

- **Focus on scalable** – Originators must bear in mind – at all points during the research process – that their aim is to confirm the existence of 'well-sized' markets and segments that will enable them to (eventually) scale up. Brand equity can only be grown through scale and reach. If potential brand builders fail to find a sizable market for their idea, they would be well advised – unless they want to run a sub-scale hobbyhorse – to come up with another inspired hunch or gem of an idea.

CASE STUDY 3 – MILLER & CARTER: FINDING THE GAP
Tony Hughes

Tony Hughes (co-author of this book) is the founder and originator of Miller & Carter, the UK's fastest growing premium steakhouse brand.

Contrary to much academic commentary (which assumes a high degree of sequential analysis and planning) brands often come about opportunistically. There might be rational analysis about how and why a certain brand came about, but very often the spark that ignites the fire in multi-brand companies has arisen in a serendipitous, intuitive fashion as a solution to an 'estate portfolio' problem rather than an urge to be spontaneously creative. Take one of the most successful brands I've created – people might think that, at the time, my team and I kicked off the Miller & Carter concept following some magnificent consumer insight! Perhaps that came later – but the reason we invented the brand is far simpler than that:

- The motivation – really the main impetus behind Miller & Carter was born out of opportunism. We had just purchased [256] sites from one of our major competitors; many of these sites were failing 'value' steakhouse venues. Whilst we could fill many of these sites with brands from our existing portfolio (i.e. Harvester and Toby Restaurants), the demographics of some locations required a more aspirational solution. Although we had some (developing) premium brands that could have 'fitted' the sites, the scale of the units required an offer that would accommodate high volumes of trade to exploit the asset potential.

- The insight – our initial kernel of an idea was to substitute the 'value' steakhouse with a 'premium' steakhouse offer (there's always demand for a good steakhouse; think of Berni or Beefeater) – the trick is KISS (keep it simple stupid). Looking at the UK suburban restaurant market, we felt there was a major gap to be filled here – there was no major chain that covered this premium market segment. Our issue was – if we were going to do it – what should it look and feel like?

- The inspiration – I assembled an elite project team led by Ian Dunstall, our Marketing Director, Mark Jacobs, Operations Manager, and Tony Booth of Design Coalition. Then, knowing the US market fairly well, I briefed them to go out to the US and look at three premium restaurant operations, in particular: Houston's in Addison, Dallas and Winter Park, Orlando; and Seasons 52, in Sand Lake Drive, Orlando. I asked them to closely observe, analyse and capture their design, core operations and service culture... and when they came back we essentially simplified the operation to a premium steakhouse to make it more resilient and easier to operate. We picked Miller & Carter from the telephone directory as the most English sounding names... The brand was essentially creative plagiarism: a bundle of three ideas – American design, premium steakhouse and English name...

After opening our first prototype and three trial sites, we formulated the brand position to define with clarity the core principles of the brand, which connect it with its consumers, and to provide guidance to future 'brand stewards' for future evolution.

The functional and emotional positioning values of Miller & Carter were defined as 'simple luxury' – communicated as 'little black dress'; a clear and descriptive way of understanding the brand role... an essential element for every woman to own is a simple, elegant black dress that can be dressed up or down making it suitable for a wide range of occasions – always with style! ...

Today, Miller & Carter is cited by its current CEO as one of the company's power brands, protected from the value market 'dogfight' through a clear premium positioning. It has a broad consumer appeal, having achieved category-leading status in the local micro-markets within which it is situated. But it's fascinating to know where its origins lie – necessity certainly is the mother of invention!

2.2 Compelling Concept

Once Originators have 'sense tested' their initial idea and established that there will be a credible market need, they can turn their attention to building a compelling concept. But what does this term – compelling concept – infer? What it means is that the brand must be constructed in such a way so as to appear exciting and alluring to its target customer base. As such it must – as we argued in the introduction – be based around an attractive culinary proposition, supported by distinctive functional and emotional benefits that satisfy the needs, feelings and aspirations of both employee and customer. These will – in turn – translate into high levels of attraction, loyalty and advocacy. So how should the founder–entrepreneur's 'heroic mission' now be made tangible and translated into a viable, compelling proposition?

Concept Qualifiers

In order to construct a compelling concept that is likely to be sustainable over the longer term, it is advisable for Originators to take the following steps:

- ◘ **Define the brand's personality** – early stage brand builders must decide how the brand will 'speak' and relate to its key stakeholder constituencies (customers, staff, partners, suppliers and so forth). To this extent, it must have a clear identity, which should be expressed through a definition of its brand essence and the careful assembly of symbolic brand elements:
    - *Brand essence* – there are two ways of approaching this. Either the founder can choose four or five words 'from the heart' which

sum up what the brand stands for and what customer needs it will fulfil (for example, for Nando's: pride, passion, courage, integrity and family). Or brand builders can undertake a 'bridging process' where the key functional component of the product is linked or bridged to a relevant and credible psychological satisfaction delivered by the brand. Such a process is intended to carve out a 'clear appeal area' which encompasses an integrated bridged expression of both functional and psychological needs. This 'bridged need' is then connected to an evaluator that allows brand owners to measure delivery (see case study below).

- *Brand elements* - great thought must also go into 'elemental coherence' during the construction process; designing and commissioning the brand's name (will it be descriptive - cooking process or cuisine - or alliterative, iconographic, personified, geographic, made up etc.?), logo (visual identifier), tagline (catchphrase), graphics (shapes and patterns) etc. Are they evocative? Do they symbolise what the brand seeks to represent? Will they appeal to core customers (without offending infrequent users)?

◻ **Distinctive customer benefits** - it is important that the brand appears unique to customers, offering benefits that other brands don't. Brand builders can achieve clarity in this process by using some of the outputs from the 'bridging process' (outlined above) to define distinctive functional and emotional attributes of the brand that appeal to tangible and intangible customer requirements:
- *Functional benefits* - product-based (taste and quality) and economic (value proposition)
- *Emotional* - psychological (identity, feeling and aspiration) and sociological (affiliation, community and sociability).

◻ **Rigorous design and testing** - the concept requires violent 'stress testing' in market, where essential components of the brand are gauged against customer reaction. Designers and property agents are fully briefed about the target customers, the culinary proposition and distinctive brand essence. So what fundamental principles apply at this stage?
- *Core demographic proximity* - it is absolutely critical (as Meyer states above) that the first test unit is placed within context.

That is to say, it is in a place where it can address its intended 'serviceable market'. This might require a lot of time patiently searching for a location with the right fit. It is time well spent. Location will be a major determinant of success or failure – inattention to this fundamental requirement will mean certain failure.

- *One prototype, three trials* – unlike FMCG where goods can be produced and tested behind closed doors, food service concept testing requires customer testing in 'live' environments. But one site does not necessarily confirm or reject viability. It is highly advisable that brand builders treat their first site as a working prototype which is then trialled in three other locations that are clustered within a relatively tight geography (to minimise distance and monitoring issues). This will produce a mine of information concerning its portability.
- *Sensory cues* – now that the brand is in nascent flight, the culinary proposition can be rigorously tested. Customer reaction to the menu can be judged (especially with regard to signature dishes), customer feelings about the design, ergonomic flow and decor can be judged and the emotional responses to the concept's chain of service (comprising each 'customer touch') can be appraised. In fact, all sensory cues including colour, sound and taste can be trialled and tweaked accordingly to create a memorable customer experience.
- *Viable business model* – at this stage, brand builders can also check financial viability. Initially they will have had a projected P&L so now the key questions are: Does it stand up during live testing? What is the real rhythm of the business? Is the concept doing the covers that were anticipated and the times that were planned for? Does the average spend per head (ASPH) stack up? What is the real gearing of this business (i.e. costs as a proportion of sales)? Based on these trials what is the likely ROI of this concept going to be?

■ **Core-team capability** – establish a core team (most likely to be early enthusiasts and to display risk-taking entrepreneurial characteristics themselves) that can carry out the vital operational functions of the brand during its early stage development.

Concept Differentiators

But what sets successful Originators apart from the rest during the concept construction and testing stage?

- **Multi-disciplinary expert assistance** – what the brand builder needs to ask him-/herself right from the get go is whether s/he wants the brand to be world class or Wolverhampton class. For sure, successful Originators can put together a compelling concept through a process of sheer bloody-minded trial and error, but they would be well advised to speed it up and increase its chance of success by co-opting the help and advice of multi-disciplinary professionals (designers, cuisineurs, property specialists, marketers, financiers, operators etc.) who have had experience in assisting the set-up of successful food service concepts in the past.
- **Flexible mindset** – during these important initial stages, the Originator will be exposed as having many false pre-conceptions. For instance, his/her idea of the core addressable market and/or main competitive set might turn out to be wrong. Also things that s/he believed would be sacrosanct within the brand (i.e. specific 'hero' dishes and/or specific KVIs/price points) might turn out to be false. Successful brand builders must have a passionate guiding vision – this is what enables them to bulldoze obstacles and overcome miss-steps – but they must also have a flexible mindset that enables them to play the game as it unfolds in front of them, dispassionately slaughtering wrongly held 'sacred cow' prejudices and beliefs if needs be.
- **Good investors** – one factor that is absolutely essential to the project's success is the presence of a line of funding provided by good investors. That is to say, those that are providing the financial backing for the new concept have high liquidity and – whilst understanding the risks – believe in the Creator and share his/her vision. Good investors take a long-term view and are tolerant of missteps and mistakes; as long as they can see – in these early stages – that they are not throwing good money after bad!
- **Internalise the brand** – at these early stages, the brand builder is focused upon building a compelling concept that has traction in the external market. However, during this process of concept construction, s/he must simultaneously contemplate how the brand will be made 'salient' by being brought alive internally. The functional and emotional benefits that the brand offers for customers must be

mirrored by a set of clear benefits for staff that will energise and come to personify the brand (see Vibrant Culture, below).

CASE STUDY 4 – **BURGER & LOBSTER AND CABANA: CREATING COMPELLING CONCEPTS**
Misha Zelman and Jamie Barber

Burger & Lobster is a fast-growing monoproduct concept (favourably reviewed by some commentators as the best type of 'premium fast food') that, having successfully launched in London in 2012, is now being franchised internationally outside of its UK and US heartlands. In this mission statement, its founder, Misha Zelman, describes the 'big idea' underpinning the brand.

Monoproduct Manifesto

I believe that a restaurant with just one dish on the menu can be popular – and financially successful. Want to know why? Read on and comment on my Manifesto.

Monoproduct Philosophy

The concept of a monoproduct restaurant is a reflection of fairly common global processes on a particular market place, which are linked to many aspects of modern life. These processes are the result of rapidly developing technologies, which accelerate change and stimulate consumption. Manufacturers offer all they have and by so doing provoke in consumers a defensive reaction against the limitless choice and chaos produced by it. There is a need for a new service which can be called 'making choices for you'.

In Medieval times, in so-called 'restaurants', there had never been a huge menu for quite objective reasons (primitive food technology): it simply could not have existed. Nowadays we consciously try to make menus less extensive. There is a theory that civilisation develops in cycles. In regard to consumption, we are also going back to where it all started. Truly global craftsmen are appearing who offer a small choice of unique products – just one phone, one tablet, etc. After having opened my first monoproduct restaurant 'Burger & Lobster' (*Yes, I know... TWO products!*) in London at the beginning of this year, I've confirmed with my own experience: this trend is applicable on the global restaurant market as well.

Today globalisation, cosmopolitanism and tolerance are eroding national borders. This allows us, the Russians, to open steak houses in London and Zurich, where American meat is cooked in Spanish ovens – and to make them both popular and successful. I'm not saying I've invented the bicycle; no one is saying that there had never been establishments similar to monoproduct restaurants before. There have always been pizzerias, dumpling bars (*Rus. Pelmennaya*) or chebureks-houses (Central Asian) but they all existed outside of the global competition that exists today and they force us to create a 'cult' of one dish and do our best to make it perfect.

Monoproduct Contents

I'd like to offer for your attention a number of criteria which define a monoproduct restaurant:

- A monoproduct restaurant is focused on one dish; other dishes (side dishes or desserts) are only a necessary distraction
- The quality of preparation of this dish is as close to ideal as possible
- The process of preparation of this dish and other technologies are brought to perfection
- The atmosphere (interior design, waiters) focuses the consumer on enjoying the food
- The financial model is extremely stable: energy consumption and staff costs are reduced and the division of labour allows for the raising of productivity.

Monoproduct Goals

- To offer the customer a dish second to none, a one off
- To offer the customer a new algorithm: the customer knows which dish he or she wants to taste today and accordingly chooses the restaurant in which it is best prepared, not vice versa
- To make a restaurant famous and popular by providing supreme quality of food preparation
- To create competition with multiproduct restaurants
- To create competition among monoproduct restaurants and contribute to the development of this format.

Cabana is a fast-growing UK chain of Brazilian Barbecues which currently has 10 units. Here, its founder, Jamie Barber, explains how he conceived his original idea and the key characteristics to which he attributes his chain's early success.

In my early career I was a corporate lawyer and one of my clients (Roger Moore of Bond fame, no less) mentioned that his son wanted to open up a restaurant concept. It sparked an idea (to open an upscale hospitality business in Mayfair) and a lifelong passion. Over time I set up a number of other successful premium businesses which I built up before eventually selling on – a practice I found to be quite successful. One of my acquaintances – David Ponte – had opened a Brazilian concept called Mocoto in Knightsbridge that had attempted to capture classic Brazilian cuisine; but it was a little before its time in many respects and he had to close it. However, it was a great idea. I had just sold a number of businesses and was looking for something with real growth potential, so I kept pestering him: 'why don't we have a go at that thing with skewers?' We now have 10 sites, having launched our first one at the (then brand new) Westfield Stratford shopping centre back in 2008. To what do I attribute our early success?

- ◘ **Focused and differentiated** – Cabana has really found a space in the market. I remember my sister, after she had graduated from university, complaining that she didn't want to meet her friends surrounded by school kids in Nando's. There was a gap for what I term the 'transitional generation' for a great social space with great food. There is nothing in the market that comes close to matching our focus upon delivering Brazilian barbecue skewers in a vibrant South American environment.
- ◘ **Authentic** – customers can see through concepts that have been contrived in Boardrooms! My business partner and I researched the brand essence by going out to Brazil, deconstructing the whole concept and making it 'fit' for a UK casual dining format (waiters with waistcoats wouldn't really work over here). Our mission is to 'lift people's spirits', 'blowing them away with taste' and 'transport[ing] them to Brazil'. We work hard to connect people to the brand, for example with the *Cabana Cookbook*, which has sold over 60,000 copies and been published in six different languages. It's really important that our employees understand, buy into and exemplify the brand, and we have taken a number of them on trips out to Brazil to really feel and touch the culture we're aspiring to replicate.
- ◘ **Scalability** – one thing I had learnt from my earlier ventures is that

you must build a brand to be scalable from day one. I'm a believer that in order to achieve 'proof of concept', you need to test it out in two sites in order to determine whether it is the concept or site that is actually the main determinant of success. You must also set out as you intend to proceed. At Cabana, we deliberately put in an expensive IT/EPoS infrastructure from day one that – although 'over spec'd' for a few units – would be 'fit for purpose' for a large chain. We also deliberately built small, well-kitted-out kitchens which would only take three people to operate – even in busy peak shifts – so that we wouldn't build unnecessary costs into the model (big kitchens encourage 'menu creep' and excessive manning).

- **Flexibility** – another thing we have done from the get go is to recognise that we need to be flexible in terms of how and where we can fit the brand within particular locations. Our site acquisition targets include retail malls (where we look for 3–6k sq ft units), 'transformational high streets' (neglected high streets that require new energy) and 'high octane' locations (such as Canary Wharf and Soho). This means we must be flexible in our approach to scale and design; something that is highly important if we are going to rapidly expand.

2.3 Vibrant Culture

Food service concepts require what academics call a strong 'service culture personality'; that is to say, the staff come to personify the brand in the eyes of the customer. Hence, brand builders might have a compelling culinary concept with a great market positioning but it will wither and fail unless it is underpinned by a vibrant service culture! In effect, a culture is an ideological 'soft control' mechanism which enables the founder to exert control through shared commitment, buy-in and belief. In the initial stages of brand construction, the culture and tone of the brand will be set by the Originator who exemplifies the pioneering spirit of the endeavour. At this stage, s/he will consciously or unconsciously establish – through actions and behaviours – the shared values, beliefs, norms and customs which will shape and pervade 'the way in which things are done around here'. Apocryphal myths, legends, heroes, icons and stories feed and perpetuate the organisation's culture and identity; providing both inspiration and guidance to employees as to what 'good looks and feels like'. But what are the main qualifiers and differentiators with regards to creating a vibrant culture in a new food service venture?

Cultural Qualifiers

It is our strongly held belief (see Introduction) that in order to build a strong, vibrant service culture in food service brands, Originators should devote as much time to attending to the needs, feelings and aspirations of employees as they do to those of customers. This can result in real competitive advantage. As has been previously stated, the hospitality sector is caricatured as a 'constrained choice industry' or 'refuge sector' offering poor wages, insufficient training and development, with a repressive and demanding long-hours culture. What great food service brands do from the off is create a great culture in which talented people want to work and then hire staff with service personalities at all levels of the organisation – placing particular emphasis on animating front-line 'customer touching' employees:

◘ **Attend to the cultural web** – strong cultures comprise a *holistic* set of components which instil a sense of confidence and well-being amongst employees. The Cultural Web Model in Figure 2 (Johnson and Scholes 1993) illustrates the main elements that contribute to building the cultural 'software of the mind' within brands, providing a useful checklist and reference point for Creators.

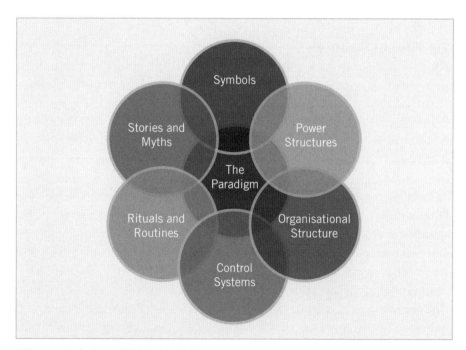

Figure 2 **Cultural Web Model**

We believe this model offers some guidance to Originators on the main (integrated) artefacts of culture – useful because culture is often viewed as an abstract, intangible construct. But how should Creators either consciously or inadvertently enliven each component?

- *The paradigm* – the paradigm at the centre of the web comprises the binding core purpose of the brand (its essence, promise, benefits and values). This encapsulates the brand's 'central belief system' and 'the way in which we do things around here'. Cultural paradigms are idiosyncratic to brands due to influences such as positioning, founder vision and history. To this extent they are inimitable (i.e. can't be copied) so are a source of great competitive advantage. The core purpose of the brand should then be reflected, reinforced and buttressed by six key factors about which Originators would do well to ask themselves a number of questions.
- *The six key factors* –
  i. *Healthy rituals and routines* – do we have positive formal and informal rituals and routines for work? Have we modelled and instilled good habits, a strong work ethic and protocols that are well understood and accepted?
  ii. *Meritocratic symbols* – what are the main artefacts of status (such as job titles, offices and perks) in our brand? Who gets what? Are we going to appear meritocratic or look greedy and despotic?
  iii. *Heroic stories* – what are the apocryphal legends, tales and narratives regarding our heroic successes or failure? How do we disseminate them? How can we bring them alive as a driving force for excellence and high achievement? How can we use them as cautionary tales for arrogance and/or over exuberance?
  iv. *Agile organisational structure* – how are we going to organise our key functions? To what extent are 'enabling' staff detached from the operational line? Are we providing 24/7 support to our customer-facing employees?
  v. *Sensible control systems* – what do we punish or reward around here? Do we rely excessively on micro-management and tough measures for all activities? Are we sure that controls are in place to make sure all our operations are (at the very least) safe and legally compliant?

vi. Democratic power structures – who wields ultimate power in this organisation? Is it stifling or empowering? Does it add value to the customer experience or not? How empowered are our customer-facing staff to instantly rectify customer problems or mollify complaints?

◻ **Instil front-line service culture** – great food service brands aim for consistently high levels of service *performance* in heterogeneous circumstances. But what are the main drivers behind great service performance? Obviously, the brand needs to be set up correctly in the first instance, possessing a compelling concept and vibrant culture. The latter will be strengthened if there is an unambiguous and explicit focus upon hiring front-line staff with great 'service personalities' that are able to bring the brand to life in front of the customer. Our Service Culture Wheel (SCW) in Figure 3 is a representation of the key elements that lead to a positive service culture at unit level within branded chains. Its sequential stages represent the various interdependent attributes of unit-level service cultures that will result in satisfying/memorable service experiences for guests/users – ultimately resulting in retention, loyalty, advocacy and new user recruitment, resulting (hypothetically) in higher sales and a better reputation.

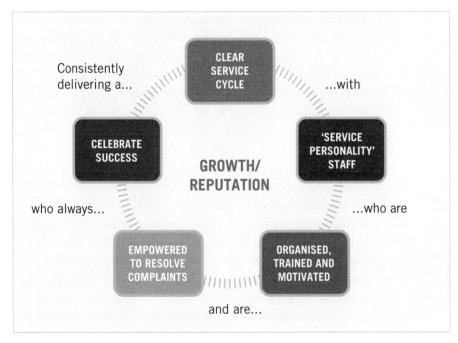

Figure 3 **Service Culture Wheel**

In essence, the SCW highlights five interlinked stages involved in constructing a successful unit-level service culture which should provoke specific checks for brand builders:

- *Clear service cycle* – the chain of service (customer 'touches' from welcome to exit) should be simple and easily understood by service providers involved at key moments of the customer order-fulfilment process. *Check*: is our chain of service clear and documented in *simple terms* for front-line service providers?
- *Service personality staff* – staff should be recruited into service-based businesses on the basis of 'will' – not purely 'skill'. Staff who gain pleasure from serving others and working as a team can be trained to despatch the technical aspects of the role within service organisations. Recruiting for 'emotional contagion' is more important than hiring for pure technical ability. *Check*: are our GMs and their management teams hiring 'service personalities'?
- *Organised, trained and motivated* – following immersion, staff should be trained, developed, deployed, rewarded and resourced with the tools to do the job to expedite their duties with passion and efficiency. Their *core* job 'purpose' should be made clear and unambiguous (e.g. waitress: 'to make customers happy') *Check*: are we organising /motivating/training our service providers appropriately?
- *Empowered to resolve complaints* – immediate on-the-spot rectification of problems or service breakdowns will not only (in most cases) exceed customer expectations, it will result in positive perceptions about the brand/product *Check*: are our service providers aware of our rectification protocol – are they properly empowered/equipped to resolve issues on the spot?
- *Celebrate success* – post-session recognition of great service moments either individually or on a team basis will reinforce and bolster positive service behaviours in the future. Do we celebrate WOW! service moments with the team? *Check*: are we recognising team members with rewards that they can show or boast about to their friends and families (thereby increasing their levels of pride and self-esteem)?

■ **Animate behaviours** – as intimated by both models above, Originators should seek to animate front-line behaviours through a number of techniques and interventions. These can be *re-cast* a different way according to the guiding model of the book as 'the provision of *distinctive* functional and emotional benefits that attract, retain and enthuse staff about the brand':

- *Functional/extrinsic benefits* – the costs associated with working in hospitality (unsociable hours, dealing with tricky customers, displaying enthusiastic behaviour, despatching difficult and/or mundane tasks) must be compensated for with appropriate benefits. So-called functional/extrinsic benefits (base line 'satisfiers' that may not be 'motivators' in themselves but certainly create the conditions for intrinsic motivators to work) must be put in place to ensure the attraction and retention of quality personnel. Too often, food service business owners attempt to get away with paying the minimum and providing poor working conditions. How do the best stand out? What distinctive functional benefits do they provide that satisfy basic extrinsic needs?
  - Basic pay, incentives (including tips) and bonuses that exceed local market rates
  - Guaranteed shift hours and job security
  - Generous benefits (including discounted meals and drinks on-shift, proper shift breaks, adequate holidays that can be taken anytime with proper advance warning, maternity pay, health cover assistance, sickness cover, free stock, company discount card etc.)
  - Great working conditions and tools to do the job (clean restrooms, personal lockers for belongings, adequate uniform provision, appropriate machinery, technology and facilities to get the job done etc.).

- *Emotional/intrinsic benefits* – once basic, lower-order needs have been satisfied, Originators can address 'intrinsic' motivators (those that stimulate higher-order feelings and aspirations). These can be sub-divided into two areas: psychological and sociological stimulants.
  - Psychological stimulants
    i. Meaning – giving employees a sense of higher purpose and the belief that they are doing 'worthwhile' work. This is articulated through the brand's core purpose (i.e. 'bring joy', 'make customers happy so that they return again and again', 'we care for you so that you care for our customers').

It is reinforced by the cultural artefacts referred to in the Cultural Web Model (see Figure 2 on page 38).

ii. Leadership – providing inspiring leadership both centrally and locally that embodies and exemplifies the brand essence and values. Effective leaders will communicate and 'signal' the following:

- Clear vision and direction – a sense of where the brand is heading and what it is trying to achieve.

- High levels of trust – through coherent decision making, consistency, honesty, transparency and offering opportunities for involvement, participation and consultation to improve the business. Also, effective leaders will be admired for 'catching staff doing it right!' rather than just focusing upon the negatives.

- Local empowerment – due to the heterogeneous nature of food service (the differing requirements and expectations of each customer), effective leaders must grant a degree of local autonomy to service providers to ensure they can react appropriately to (reasonable) customer requests. Their ability to respond to spontaneous demands and/or rectify issues quickly will have a huge impact on how the brand is perceived and used. Also, granting some allowance for individual service providers to have a 'signature expression' at some point during the service cycle will reinforce employee's sense of freedom and empowerment.

iii. Progressive HRM – in addition to these behaviours, effective leaders will sanction progressive HRM (human resource management) practices and policies which will positively impact employee feelings and aspirations:

- Attraction/immersion – a rigorous process that selects people with service personalities (through creative job advert copy, on-site auditions, on-the-job trials and sign off by other team members). Immersion programmes that provide in-depth induction into the brand and role (with face-to-face and online education and instruction). Employee attachment to the brand begins at this early stage – getting it right will lock in 'hearts and minds' quickly.

- Meritocratic development – effective brand leaders 'have an ever-expanding expectation of their people's abilities'. They are able to use great programmes and interventions (coaching, mentoring, buddying) to enhance the skills and capabilities of their people. Development programmes will be particularly prized and valued by employees if they are formally accredited and nationally recognised.
- Tangible recognition – in addition to accredited programmes, tangible recognition mechanisms (certificates, badges, letters, photographs, vouchers etc.) that enable employees to show their peers, friends and family the fruits of their achievements – boosting their levels of ego, self-esteem and pride in the organisation – are highly effective motivators.
- Equitable policies and practices – HRM practices such as performance reviews, incentive schemes, grievance/disciplinary procedures, and career progression 'rules' that are perceived to be fair and equitable will also stimulate positive responses from employees.

○ Sociological stimulants – in addition to these psychological stimulants that address individual employee feelings and aspirations, Originators also need to address their employees' basic human need for affiliation and social interaction. Humans generally gain fulfilment from being part of, and contributing to, a 'clan' – and fortunately, food service is the ultimate 'team game'! Brand builders can satisfy needs for affiliation through a number of means, not least:
  - Promoting local teamship – through personification and identification (shift and unit), recognition and awards
  - Promoting brand 'membership' – through regional and national meetings, ceremonies and conferences
  - Promoting local community involvement – through 'giving company time' to employees to contribute to their local communities (fund raising, lending practical skills to local projects etc.). Encouraging teams to 'get involved locally' not only raises brand awareness and reputation, it also increases team-member bonding and

levels of self-worth (particularly amongst socially minded Generation Ys).

Cultural Differentiators

The outcome of Originators applying some or all of the principles outlined above in the early stages of brand development should result in positive employee behaviours (i.e. attachment, effort and advocacy). But what sets successful brand builders apart from the rest during the process of creating a vibrant culture?

- **External and internal salience** – it is important to reiterate that there must be absolute salience between the brand essence, promise and values for both external positioning purposes and internal alignment. They are not mutually interdependent. This inter-connectedness will drive purposeful and intentional employee behaviours that will generate the outcomes that the brand leadership requires. However, Originators must ensure that they put in place all the appropriate 'cultural mechanisms and cues' that will underpin and reinforce the brand's core purpose. Success is achieved when internal behaviours become self-regulating: that is to say, when employees take it upon themselves to act as brand guardians in circumstances or situations that threaten to hurt the brand.
- **'Elite' philosophy** – it is our belief that the best brands create an aura and sense of specialness amongst employees. Great leaders propagate a passionate commitment to, and a belief in, virtues of being consistently excellent. They aspire to make followers feel that they are part of an elite team, far better than their competitive set. Making people feel that they are involved in a 'great mission' with outstanding colleagues will instil strong feelings of attachment and belonging. Mediocrity within the brand 'clan' will not be tolerated. Care must be taken, however, that this philosophy does not transmogrify into misplaced arrogance and complacency!
- **Countercultural transcendence** – Originators must ensure that brand values overcome countercultural threats in both international contexts (when they might extend the brand abroad later) and/or amongst migrant workers (in a domestic context now as they start up the operation). What do we mean by this? Often 'developed world' brands have ethical, participative and emancipative values that do not fit in some international contexts. Some societies – due to historical

and geo-political reasons – display an acceptance or preference for high levels of self-protective leadership, masculine dominance, covering up (due to fear of retribution), relation-led patronage and accountability avoidance. This is problematic for brands both attempting to expand in these territories and when engaging migrant labour from these areas into their domestic operations. What should they do to ensure that their brand's values transcend contrarian mores, norms and beliefs? First, they should recognise that it is a real issue – many companies don't! Second, they must ensure that they recruit against their values (checking for alignment but also signalling to prospective staff that 'this is the way we do things around here'). Third, their immersion programmes must inculcate and reinforce the brand's values system. Fourth, brand leadership must model the values on a day-to-day basis. Fifth, reward and punishment systems must deliver 'values cues' for either acceptable or unacceptable behaviours.

◆ **'Leader cult' avoidance** – this chapter has focused upon creating a food service brand, a process which – by its very nature – is reliant upon the immense passion, energy and borderline obsessive behaviour of its creator. What new brands must try to avoid, however, is framing themselves completely around the Originator, fashioning a sort of 'cult of personality'. Why? In order to grow, the brand will require leaders at all levels of the organisation who must think for themselves. Total dependency on the whims and wishes of one person will lead to paralysis as the brand gets larger, unless decision making is devolved and spread out. Additionally, at some point the founder will move on or be replaced – if the brand is totally built around them a large vacuum will occur, possibly resulting in decline (because in the absence of instructions from the 'dear leader', nobody knows what to do next). The brand DNA and its 'archaeology' thus need to be disseminated and understood by as many people as possible if it is to survive and flourish as a viable entity long after the founder has departed.

CASE STUDY 5 – **HACHÉ AND GIGGLING SQUID: CREATING A VIBRANT CULTURE**

Berry Casey and Andy Laurillard

Founded in 2004, Haché is a London-based premium burger restaurant chain with six sites. Here the founder, Berry Casey, describes the culture that he and his wife have instilled in the brand, which they believe to be a vital ingredient of its success.

After a successful career in advertising, we founded and ran a couple of concepts – the Camden Crepe Company and Bagels Already – which furnished us with many lessons when we came up with the idea for an upmarket burger restaurant in the mid-noughties. Central to our insights was the need to be differentiated from the competition both in terms of quality and price. But just as important was the culture of the brand required to underpin the brand's personality... So how have we ensured that our service and environment are distinctive from 'canteen' and 'better' burger concepts that have challenged us over the past ten years?

- ◻ **Central belief** – at Haché (which means 'to chop' in French) our philosophy is 'j'aime Haché, j'aime la vie' ('love Haché, love life'). We are in the business of *making people happy* – both staff and customers. Yes, the core strength of the brand is derived from obsessive attention to detail to the core product (that we don't undermine by 'trading on price'); but it is the philosophy that underpins our brand that our competitors can't copy.
- ◻ **Story** – when we started up the brand, we had a very clear vision about what our brand must be. At the time GBK was the clear market leader and we took a chance by opening our first site in an off-pitch location in Camden. At first we didn't know whether or not Haché would work and over time we have faced not only the challenges of launching but also surviving the 2008–14 recession and the onslaught of new competition during 2014–15. But 'don't panic, Mr Mainwaring!' We survived start-up by getting rave reviews in the *Guardian* and *Time Out* (culminating in being awarded Burger Restaurant of the Year) – this put 25% on the trade. The recession was weathered as we offered a 'low spend per head' in chic surroundings. Presently we are seeing the competition off – retaining loyal regulars – because we haven't compromised our principles. This story resonates with both staff and customers.

- **Icons** – my wife and I are very much fans of minimalist design with a 'chic twist'. Indeed, my wife has been the inspiration for many of the design icons of the Haché brand such as the 'stripped back' interior juxtaposed against chandeliers and fairy lights. The ambience and décor of our restaurants means that we are set apart from 'canteen lookalikes' – it is a place where people like coming to work and couples and friends like to socialise.
- **Hierarchy** – our brand is like a family and, as the song goes, 'the love you take is equal to the love you make'. A happy team means a happy ambience – we have a very low staff turnover and all our general managers have been promoted from within. The skills and talents of our staff are amazing (most of whom are aged 18–35) – they are well-qualified, energetic, positive people who 'get' Haché. Yes, we've had to professionalise and standardise systems as we've grown (taking on more people to support the brand) but we have kept our formula for maintaining team spirit.
- **Control** – the values of our brand keep attitudes and behaviours on track but technological innovation has meant that these days you can view restaurant transactions and till takings from anywhere in the world – daily and hourly! So we have a pretty good up-to-the minute feel for how the business is doing. If we have a problem, it becomes immediately apparent.
- **Rituals** – this brand is all about having fun. The brand's sense of humour is expressed in billboard advertising at tube stations near our branches and on social media. We have an incredibly loyal following who we reward through our Société Haché loyalty card and by putting on different specials every month ('vive le difference!'). However, we are aware that we can't stand still: as we have grown in confidence we have taken on bigger sites (our newest one in Chelsea is bigger and bolder and doing extremely well) and developed our interior design. But we are not focussed on a breakneck speed of expansion; rather, on continuing to be innovative – and remembering that it's all about the brand – its distinctiveness, reputation and trust – evolving the brand in keeping with its core philosophy: 'j'aime Haché, j'aime la vie'!

Giggling Squid is a successful Thai tapas chain that currently has ten sites. Here, the founder, Andy Laurillard, reflects on the consequences of a cultural mismatch, as experienced when the brand took over premises vacated by a 'downsizing' national brand.

Although I was working in marketing, my wife and I had significant experience running a Thai restaurant in Brighton called 'mai ped, ped, ped' when another site was offered to us for a proverbial 'box of cornflakes'. After brainstorming the name – my son came up with Wriggling Fish that over a bottle of wine became Giggling Squid – we opened our first unit that was based on providing greater accessibility to Thai cuisine comprising English language menus and a stripped-down, contemporary design.

During the Giggling Squid expansion journey from our first premises in Hove, we have encountered a number of issues such picking a wrong site (which seriously stalled our wider roll-out plans), encountering listed-building issues and being quickly surrounded by casual dining competitors in key locations. However, the distinctiveness and quality of our offer allied to the fact that we have been prepared to customise our offer in various location (i.e. variable/seasonal pricing, different wine menus etc.) has kept up our forward momentum. Our latest unit in Salisbury is located in a prime location (challenging our assumptions that we are an off-pitch operator that can only afford secondary sites) and is 'shooting the lights out'. We now have a 'market grid' that details key locational requirements and we now know exactly where our target towns and sites are. But one thing that has sustained and underpinned our growth is **our culture**. In one site acquisition, however, it all went horribly wrong for a while…

If I was to define our culture, I would say that our main guiding principles are:
- **Keep it tight** – we have strong values that are understood and bought into by all of our people, top to bottom. Our estate is purposefully located only two hours from our house in the London commuter belt, enabling my wife and I to get around, reinforcing messages and standards.
- **Cooperate** – we stress cooperation as a cornerstone of the brand, something that is highly necessary when you are refining and rolling out a new concept.
- **Share the work** – hospitality is hard work, but this is made easier if everybody pitches in to do whatever is required to delight customers.
- **Share the rewards** – we really look after our people: we need to win in the Thai labour market! Our kitchen staff are on good pay and benefits. Also BOH and FOH share the rewards – in particular, tipping.

We realised how important these cultural dynamics are when we took over a premises from a major chain in a 'theatrical tourist' hotspot town. It was a really good pitch and we assumed that it would take off like a train. However, it was a car crash in terms of cultural differences. The staff we inherited just did not get it... It took us quite some time – by redeploying staff into the unit from other locations – to get the micro-culture of the unit right... It was a good lesson for us – we now have a much greater understanding of the type of people that we prefer – *attitude is so much more important than skills and experience...* As the organisation grows and we put in a supporting infrastructure – we have taken on an Ops Director and Ops Managers in the last twelve months – it is important these new hires also buy into our culture, which is one of the main defining reasons for our sustained success. This is an extremely successful brand now, with REAL momentum – but like all successes – it has not been without its road bumps...

Final Thoughts

This chapter has outlined the activities that successful Originators need to undertake during the brand-creation stage. It has argued that *first*, there is a requirement for intensive *research* into the viability of their initial hunch (through sense testing a market gap and assessing needs); *second*, patient construction of a *compelling concept*; and *third*, a focus upon building an enduring and *vibrant culture* fashioned around achieving service excellence. Much reference was made during the chapter to the main architect of this endeavour, namely the founder–entrepreneur or Originator. Case studies from industry-leading founder–entrepreneurs also illuminated our insights and these contributions will be triangulated with those of other brand-leader contributions in succeeding chapters to help us distil the essence of effective brand leadership in the book's concluding Chapter 7. But for now, let's consider what makes these individuals especially unique, what leadership style they usually possess and why they are effective.

Originators are idiosyncratic individuals who are often driven by an inner need to make their mark; that is to say they have a sense of destiny and 'heroic mission'. Their passion for what they want to achieve is all consuming and might seem to others to be highly irrational, illogical and improbable in its ambition. However, it is this enthusiasm and drive which enables them to sell their vision to other parties; most notably investors, advisors and initial core team members. Their leadership style usually comprises a heady mixture of 'autocratic charisma': decisions need to be taken quickly in order to avert mini-crises in the formative stages of a brand. This in itself might foster the self-perception by the Originator and a belief amongst his/her followers that they are infallible and have a divine right to rule. This can lead to disaster when the brand enters its major growth phase and the need for systemisation might mean that the Originator is replaced by professional Accelerator-type managers.

The effectiveness of Originators, however, stems from one central insight that can be derived from the narrative and case studies of this chapter. Successful Originators are – to coin a metaphor – able to *use a microscope and telescope simultaneously*! They have the ability to focus on the 'here and now', whilst keeping an eye on the future. They can microscopically analyse the market and attend to the brand detail whilst telescopically focussing upon the long-term vision and mission. The next chapter will now consider the escalation phase of the brand, and the principal activities that the next leadership cadre – 'Escalators' – need to execute in order to maintain brand momentum.

CHAPTER 3   **Escalate**

THREE

The previous chapter referred to the origination phase of successful food service brand development. This chapter deals with the next stage which we label 'escalation', a period when the brand seeks to successfully *scale up* to achieve category-leading status. The leadership role required during this time of rapid growth differs from the previous phase. Originators who have – through their heroic vision and mission – created a compelling culinary concept with tangible and intangible benefits (for both employees and customers) now have to change their strategic orientation from one of 'chaotic start-up' to 'professional growth'. They now need to assume the role of what we call Escalators: energetic, detail-conscious systemisers who – whilst preserving the core essence of the brand – accelerate its network growth, systemise operations and drive external awareness of the brand. New investors might now be on board (after the first 'ownership flip') with highly demanding aspirations with regards to roll-out and returns. The Escalator must satisfy these expectations whilst seeking to exploit the brand's 'first mover' advantage in order to dominate its segment.

The question is whether or not Originators can transition into the Escalator role: and the answer is, generally not! Having been used to micro-managing every detail of the brand, the Originator is loath to let go; their sense of infallibility and heroic self-perception prevents them from even considering devolving some of their power and authority to other decision makers. In such circumstances, Originators are usually 'moved out' after a short 'advisory' or 'consultancy' period to help the Escalator understand the brand DNA and its archaeology. The Escalator then sets to work in transforming a fledgling concept into an engine of high-velocity growth; putting together a targeted estate strategy, systemising tasks and routines for consistency and quality purposes, bringing in new talent to give the organisation more 'depth' and driving brand awareness through a number of traditional/ contemporary media channels. These will be considered in turn after the case study below, which provides an excellent overview of the approaches and techniques applied by an outstanding Originator turned Escalator during his brand's 'scaling up' phase of development.

CASE STUDY 6 – **GIRAFFE: GROWING A SUCCESSFUL CONCEPT**
Russel Joffe

Giraffe was founded by entrepreneurs Russel and Juliette Joffe in 1998. By 2003, it had grown to nearly 50 restaurants and was bought for £48.5m by Tesco to become the lynchpin of their all-day family dining strategy. Here, Russel reflects on how he and his wife successfully grew their brand from conception to the point of exit.

How and why did we set up Giraffe?… the journey we chose was one based on a life-style to create a restaurant brand by entrepreneurs who wanted to do things differently… no less professional than a big corporation but one based on people, hospitality and wanting to give our customers something different… But what were the main factors behind its growth?

- *Experience* – my wife and I had already set up and sold a successful chain of eight sites (one of the first real all-day cafes before Café Rouge) called Café Flo… therefore, we already had experience of setting up and rolling out a successful concept…
- *Differentiation* – after selling Flo we took a break, travelling the world, taking time out with the kids… it was during this time that we came up with a gem of an idea – creating an affordable lifestyle brand based on world music and global food with a style of doing business where we wanted no barriers to how we did things… Knowing the UK casual dining scene at the time we knew if we wanted to do something it had to be a new 'niche' – something that people didn't even know they wanted! … Based on our idea, what we came up with in our first outlet in Hampstead (a location we knew well) was an 'all-day' brand (I believe in making best use of the property!) with a 'world take' on music, décor and food – San Franciscan type bacon and eggs breakfast, Sydney lunch, all-day smoothies – healthy ingredients from the best suppliers… the name Giraffe embodied what we wanted to convey: tall, exotic, fun, global…
- *Culture* – the competitive edge we created was based around our people… they personified the brand… we created a wonderful engaged team… just like great teams in sports… everybody

aligned, working together for the success of the business... We created a great experience and atmosphere for guests by employing people we wanted to work with who bought into the ethos of the brand... for us it was about giving freedom to our people to express themselves; giving them wider barriers... engaging them by being close to them 'putting our arms around nice people'... showing them that they had a future as the brand grew; being an employer that they could be proud of... recognising them at events such as our GOSCAR's where we rewarded great guest memories and experiences... Also we were highly visible founders... interacting with staff and customers... finding out what they wanted... aligning common goals... communicating the message: particularly our philosophy of how we wanted to do business – why we come to work every-day... We often said '*we happen to be in the people business serving food!*'... We lived the brand every day and this reflected what our teams were doing and this created **memories and stories** which made our customers come more often... Our culture and our hospitality were rewarded by the measured success of the brand...

- *Patient roll-out* – from our first restaurant we grew it 'one customer – one restaurant' at a time! ... we didn't go for 'big bang' solutions; it was our money at the beginning – we weren't funded like some of our corporate competitors! ... Really our site selection was more down to gut feeling; walking the streets... Market research can tell you only so much... you need to go look and see...

- *Right partners* – when we needed development capital to grow at a faster pace and were more confident to compete at a higher level with the bigger boys, we looked for new equity partners to not only provide this capital but support us with some operational board level experience in growing a brand... The discipline alone in having to have a board meeting and prepare a pack gives you the time to think about the business and the decisions you are making – and then to discuss them and be challenged by the board helps you and your business grow! ... The challenge is not to let the corporate governance interfere with the culture you have created from the beginning – the heart and soul of the business... Without that you have nothing! ... The board has to be aligned in the decisions being made and the plan you are all working to...

- *Constant challenge* – we were always questioning what the customer and our teams wanted us to be... also our relationships with suppliers had to be good ones... from securing best prices to the unit-level service required for demanding teams... driving the best price is part of it – but so is the best service... going the extra mile... But everyone has to leave the table in agreement with the way forward and the decision made at any level (operational, team, supplier negotiation, board meetings)... We were always driven by a sense of healthy paranoia, a productive sense of fear about doing things better tomorrow....

☐ *Alignment and synchronicity* – ... but in summary, I think we were successful in scaling this brand up because everybody and everything was in sync... Our backers supported us, our team loved the brand, our customers (we had 250,000 website members at one stage) loved the experience we gave them, our suppliers loved working for a growing brand... all our stakeholders were aligned... that's why we maintained our growth – everybody was on-board; we were all in it together! ... In short, alignment and having great partners is crucial (staff, customer, suppliers, local communities, shareholders etc.) and communication between all is fundamental to building a great brand from the bottom up...

3.1 Accelerate Network

During the origination stage, the concept has been proof-tested and has successfully found a viable 'place with a market space'. Its main components have been assembled and it has a distinct personality and positioning. Now it must gain 'spatial pre-emption'; that is to say it has to grow quickly to establish competitive advantage – warding off any 'me too' challengers or plagiarists. In the UK, many concepts are tested and then achieve pre-eminence in urban areas of high demographic concentration. London is a favoured 'test' location not only due to population density and disposable income (it has 12% of the UK's population but accounts for 25% of its household wealth) but also because it is perceived as a 'trend-setting' location. A concept arriving into the provinces from London benefits from the perception that, because it was conceived in one of the great capital cities of the world, it must be a 'happening brand'. However, Escalators – wherever the brand has been born and proven to work – must now make some key decisions and supervise critical activities in order to ensure the brand is rolled out successfully. Several missteps can be made at this stage of brand development which might stall its progress or kill it off completely – location being one of the main determinants of food service brand prosperity. So what are the main qualifiers and differentiators that determine whether or not the Escalator's attempts to accelerate the network will produce positive outcomes (i.e. niche dominance, high returns and long-term sustainability)?

Network Qualifiers

The base qualifiers for accelerating the brand's network successfully include selection of the appropriate business platform, a 'forensic' site profile, a sensible estate plan, a well-briefed site-finder team, a 'congruent' site development team, an expert pre-opening team and a talented opening team:

- ◘ **Appropriate platform** – the first decision that the Escalator needs to make is what operational mode is most suitable (given current returns) and/or which platform will get the brand to scale quickly without compromising its quality and consistency. Broadly speaking, there are four types of platform that can be pursued that each have their merits and downsides:
    - Managed – choosing to go totally managed (i.e. exerting direct operational control) allows the brand to 'harvest' the profit stream from the business without sharing it with a third party. This is fine if the brand is 'throwing off' sufficient revenues to support the cost of a large central overhead and capital borrowing to fund further property development. This model will not work, however, if returns from a managed platform are likely to be thin, either due to limited scale or 'managerial shirking'.
    - Franchised – alternatively, brand owners can outsource a fair degree of financial risk and get the brand to scale quickly by licensing the brand to single or multiple franchisees. Here, the intellectual property (typically the operational blueprint and design) of their standardised format is 'loaned out' for a fixed term in exchange for a fixed fee. Additional fees might also be charged for use of proprietary technology, marketing and promotions support and supply chain access. Such an approach (done well), involving the co-option of 'multiple unit' franchisees to run several sites, can really accelerate the brand's network of food service outlets quickly. Risk here lies for the owner/franchisor in the form of franchisees undermining the essence of the brand through imperfect execution (so-called

'freeriding'). Also, insufficient support to franchisees (along the lines of those promised in the licensing document) could lead to costly claims and reputational damage for the owner.

- Concessions and licensed – this approach involves the food service brand granting legal entitlement to other companies to use its brands within their own format, sometimes in the form of implants (say in department or food retail stores). The risks to the brand owner in these types of agreement are non-payment of fees, a lack of control over the general environment in which its brand might be operated (potentially diluting its brand equity) and the fact that long-term agreements might be difficult to exit, inhibiting its ability to pursue its own organic growth strategy if it wants open its own directly managed units in the local area.

- Hybrid – in the end, the Escalator may decide that a hybrid approach (i.e. managed combined with franchised and/or licensed outlets) is the most suitable way forwards, given the risk–reward ratio. S/he might conclude that due to problems caused by distance (e.g. unfamiliar international markets), idiosyncratic conditions (e.g. travel hubs) or the fact that many 'secondary' locations fail to offer attractive managed returns (e.g. market towns as opposed to large conurbations) – franchising outside the 'managed core' represents the most sensible solution to achieving optimal reach and consumer recognition for the brand. Nevertheless, retaining a number of 'prime' managed units (i.e. those with the highest absolute returns) in a 'core estate' practically demonstrates the viability of the brand to potential franchisees and licensees. Also, a managed arm also allows brand owners to retain valuable operational knowledge and the ability to experiment without impediment.

◻ **Forensic site profile** – at this stage, it is also necessary to check that the ideal site criteria (based upon insights gained from the original outlets) are correct. These 'must haves' will inform site acquisition going forwards and include: demographic profile, population density, traffic flows (e.g. passing trade caused by retail tourism, travel or office worker footfall), complementary offers (e.g. food service 'clusters'), unit size/footprint, car parking spaces, public transport networks, freehold and leasehold thresholds (including break clauses and service charges), and essential 'props' (e.g. water, nature). It is of crucial importance that, first, these criteria are right and, second, the Escalator ensures the brand adheres to them – wherever possible – without deviation. The costs (time, effort and money) of unpicking bad locational decisions have been the bugbear of many brands that have gone into 'sporadic' roll-out, only to find that they have to rationalise their estate early on in their existence!

- **Sensible estate plan** – based on these insights, a sensible estate plan that targets prime hotspots (as opposed to notspots) for the brand can be drawn up. Having 'heat mapped' various cities and regions in the UK, decisions can be made in relation to sequencing (i.e. which area is exploited first) and the projected size of estate. This understanding of how, when and where the brand is going to scale up will greatly assist resource planning (both in terms of people and capital).

- **Well-briefed site-finder team** – fast-growing brands rarely have the internal resources to do their site searching independently. In order to hunt for the right locations, it will be necessary to co-opt incentivised property agents and searchers. In addition, the appointment of pragmatic commercial lawyers who can get deals away quickly will be an important factor in the brand growth plan.

- **'Congruent' site-developer team** – having secured a pipeline of sites (that are spread out in a development schedule to give the brand time to absorb them), a site-development team comprising project managers, architects and construction personnel should work against a clear design template. It is highly desirable (although not always possible) that this virtual team should be kept together during the brand's growth spurt in order both to consistently articulate the brand essence in any project and to forge good relationships so that developments are brought in on-time and on-budget, and that learnings are absorbed and incorporated into the design as the brand is rolled out (particularly with regards to ergonomic flows, kitchen fabrication and BOH space utilisation).

- **Expert pre-opening team** – a mistake that is commonly made when brands are in heavy roll-out mode is the reliance upon existing personnel in other nearby outlets to carry out essential pre-opening tasks (i.e. set-up, recruitment, training, local marketing and so on). Our view is that in order to preserve the like-for-like sales momentum of the core estate, organisations must decouple 'business as usual' activities and brand roll-out. The negative effects of 'hollowing out' units that are in flight in order to set up new sites can result in serious quality issues which affect the brand's local reputation. Escalators must ensure that they have at their disposal a crack pre-opening team (comprising start-up GMs, service/kitchen trainers, recruiters and marketers) that get the unit off the ground. Shambolic openings will do untold damage to the brand – recovering the brand's image in the eyes of early users who have received poor experiences will be highly expensive.

◘ **Talented opening team** – the previous chapter made reference to the imperative to attract staff with service personalities who buy into and reflect the brand's values. These behavioural competencies must be augmented by technical capability; something that can be achieved through intensive on- or offsite pre-opening training. Certainly, the key leaders in the new enterprise (GM, DM, KM, hosts and shift leaders) must have undergone intensive technical immersion in other sites within the brand portfolio to gain the explicit and tacit knowledge required to operate the unit to the required brand standards.

Differentiators

But if these are the 'qualifying' tasks that Escalators must take on during the process of accelerating the brand's coverage and network, what are the differentiating factors that set apart the best from the rest?

◘ **Optimisation not maximisation** – Escalator's will undoubtedly receive intense pressure from investors on delivering site numbers. Our advice is 'less haste, more speed'! It is better to patiently optimise the estate going forwards (putting down a brand footprint in the right areas and circumstances) rather than go for forced maximisation (performing a random, scattergun land grab in order to 'get the numbers up'). For sure, the Escalator is under pressure – for the reasons outlined at the beginning of this section (first mover advantage, category leadership etc.) – to get the brand to scale as quickly as possible. The reality is, however, that Escalators who force it will roll out in haste and repent at leisure.

◘ **Hub and spoke it** – rather than spreading the brand out in an ad hoc manner, we strongly urge the creation of a sensible Estate Plan (see above). We would further advocate the desirability of entering local markets with a flagship outlet, which will act as a hub to the further cluster units that are opened nearby. Certainly, hybrid estates should consider establishing a managed 'exemplar' unit first, to act as beacon of best practice to franchise stores that are opened in close proximity.

- ◘ **Beware of cannibalisation** - obviously, Escalators must take care that units within the estate are not cannibalising one another (i.e. eroding sales and margins by being too close). This error is commonly made by franchisors who 'gorge' within local markets by placing units and territories on top of one another, increasing their share of royalties and fees but destroying the returns of their existing franchisees. We would make the further point that Escalators operating within multi-brand organisations must also be cognisant of the effect of opening new sites next to other company-owned brands. Will such a move prove to be negative or positive? Brand architecture will dictate the degree to which there is separation between the concepts (meaning little cross-over and competitive threat); however, when two brands from the same segment, serving the same demographic collide, the outcomes for the multi-brand owner can prove extremely costly.

- ◘ **Adaptability and flexibility** - as the brand proceeds through the process of roll-out and growth, the Escalator and his/her team will learn far more about how the brand can better address customer needs, feelings and aspirations. These learnings should be incorporated into the design brief and (if possible) retro-fitted into the existing estate. In addition, the Escalator should keep an open mind on format sizes and be prepared to 'flex' the brand 'up or down' given the fact that the space that they will be able to secure for the brand will be rarely 'symmetrical'. This does not fly in the face of the advice we have given on the need to adhere to strict site criterion as long as the core essence of the brand is preserved and articulated in *all* locations.

- ◘ **Talent, talent, talent!** - a brand's growth will not be sustained without the relentless attraction of talent at all levels of the organisation to perpetuate the brand's momentum. Early recruits into the brand might have been poached by other start-ups, leaving gaps in capability. Other 'first starters' in the organisation might not have the capacity to grow with the company – given its increasing size and complexity – and consequently might need to be shipped out. The fact is, the Escalator really has to be a talent cheerleader – acting almost as a proxy Chief Talent Officer – during this growth phase, in order to accelerate the brand's scale and network.

CASE STUDY 7 – **DRAKE & MORGAN: ROLLING IT OUT**
Jillian McLean

Jillian McLean is the founder of Drake & Morgan, a London-based bar group. After an extremely successful launch in 2008, the brand now has eight sites (with a ninth pending at Kings Cross at the time of writing) generating a turnover of circa £25m with an EBITDA of £3.2m. During the next phase of its development it aims to reach approximately twenty to twenty-five units with a turnover of £70m and an EBITDA of £10m. Jillian has vast experience of the sector, having previously run some of the UK's fastest-growing brands.

Having successfully launched our concept, our attention has turned more recently to addressing its next stage of development, namely, scaling the brand up through a targeted roll-out plan. As its founder, with new investors on board, I have had to spend a great deal of time wrestling with a conundrum – how do we successfully 'scale up' the brand without losing its 'core' momentum? Based on my role here and my leadership experience rolling-out brands for corporates in the past, it is my view that – in addition to all the obvious activities and tasks – the following 'props' will be absolutely critical in effecting a successful roll-out for Drake & Morgan:

1. **'B-to-C' team** – whilst we have had a great team that has got us from A to B in our journey, through creation and start-up, we have had to spend a lot of time recruiting people with roll-out skills and experience that can get us through the next stage... Our first phase of development was characterised by energy, passion and a can-do attitude; this current phase requires more of a planning and organisational mindset (without undermining the brand essence)... In addition, we have had to be quite ruthless in making sure that business does not tail off in our original sites through distractions posed through openings elsewhere...

2. **Robust service platform** – due to my corporate background, our business systems were relatively finely tuned and templated from day one... However, our new investors, quite rightly, challenged us to ensure that our service model was replicable as we scaled up... Working with Pragma (a consultancy specialising in service delivery), we have simplified the customer service model by reducing the number of 'touch points' within the customer journey... This simplification will lead to greater consistency of execution from our teams and clarity of understanding from our customers as we move

forwards... Sometimes as a founder, you need to step back – certainly during the roll-out phase – and question: how can we do things better, faster, slicker?... and you must be prepared to discard what you initially thought were 'sacred cows' to make the brand more fit for roll-out (AGAIN without compromising the essence of the brand!)...

3. **Trend/density tracking** – of course, we have done a lot of analysis on our current sites to define a robust 'site-finding template' (demographics, footfall requirements, building aesthetics, scale of unit etc.)... We have also made great efforts to understand NOT only where our market is *now* but also *where it is going to*! ... We've done a lot of work on demographic trends with McCann Erikson... also GVA Grimley has helped us look at footfalls and densities in London... Customer traffic is constantly shifting: we need to understand transport hub plans, office development proposals and local improvement initiatives – this is where new 'exploitable' markets and customer flows will exist in the future...

4. **Landlord–tenant relationships** – when we have located prospective sites it is also crucial that we create great relationships with landlords, principal tenants and developers... We have got to understand what their needs are and how we can pitch successfully for landmark sites... In 2008, we were on a shortlist of one when we pitched; now we can be up against nearly ten rival concepts to get the best locations... We have to ensure – certainly in office locations – we are perceived as being of high value-added to landlords/developers like Land Securities and Heron... and really wanted by adjacent principal tenants like the large media and hi-tech companies that rent the dominant space... We must emphasise our all-day proposition, quality positioning and value-led characteristics (within a broader upmarket context) to make sure they want us, time and again! ...

5. **Concept flexibility** – over time we have developed a systemised 'turn-key' approach to developing sites (12 week build and fit-out, two weeks pre-opening training followed by a soft launch etc.)... But we must always retain a degree of flexibility in two respects... First, when we open a new site, because 35% of our business is pre-booked, we find out pretty quickly customers' likes and dislikes... This enables us to go back in to reset a few things; which is fine because our concept runs on an 85% fixed, 15% flexible philosophy... Second, given the space constraints we are faced with, we have proof tested smaller formats which – while maintaining the essence of the brand – will enable us to access far more site opportunities going forwards...

As the founder of this brand with a great deal of influence from my sister Amanda who is based in San Francisco – whose perspectives and knowledge derived from west coast American dining have been a critical ingredient of our success – I am conscious we have entered a new 'acceleration' phase of brand development following 'origination'... This has meant that I have had to adopt a different approach, transitioning from a Creator into an Escalator role... This has been made easier by virtue of the fact that I have done this role before in my corporate career... The factors I have cited above will be key components of our success going forwards...

3.2 Systemise Organisation

One of the major roles of the Escalator is – in tandem with professionalising the roll-out process – to systemise the routines and tasks of the brand WITHOUT DILUTING THE BRAND'S VALUES AND ESSENCE. During the creation phase of the brand's life, the Originator will have made a stab at introducing processes and policies intended to maintain product quality and consistency of standards. However, broadly speaking – because of the chaotic start-up circumstances surrounding the launch phase of the brand – standards were most likely maintained by the Originator him- or herself through a process of hands-on checking/monitoring and assertive behavioural modelling. This style of controlling operations cannot be maintained during the accelerated growth stage. Order needs to be instilled into the organisation in the form of scalable procedures and systems. An organisation is what the term implies: an ordered, purposeful assembly of hard and soft resources, shaped and aligned to produce assured outcomes. What the Escalator needs to do at this stage of the growth cycle is build an integrated structure that can execute the core tasks of the brand, underpinned by robust systems and processes that are subject to accurate measurement for performance improvement purposes. However, when building an organisational infrastructure, the Escalator must be careful that s/he doesn't destroy the raison d'être and cultural heart of the brand through excessive bureaucratisation and compliance.

Organisational Qualifiers

As stated, the three major tasks the Escalator has to perform during this phase are: to build a coherent structure; to introduce (or reinforce) robust systems and processes; and to ensure accurate measurement systems are put in place to provide conformance and delivery. Let's consider each of these in turn:

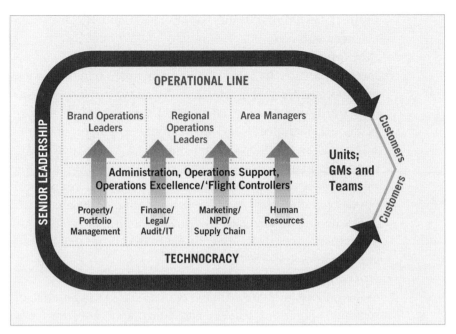

Figure 4 **Internal Value Chain Model**

□ **Integrated structure** – our Internal Value Chain Model (Figure 4) illustrates best-practice food service brand architecture.

Essentially, this model highlights the interlocking functions within a typical food service brand. It illustrates how internal functions prop up and feed into the operational line and how *all* elements of the structure should be aligned behind the main point of direct customer interface – namely, the units populated by GMs and their service-providing teams. The Escalator needs to address the five core elements of the model:

- *Strategic leadership* – these *strategic decision makers* are responsible for the strategic direction of the firm, macro-resource allocation and external stakeholder management. As the arrows on the IVCM indicate, successful food service brands generally have strategic leaders who are 'in' the business – reaching down and touching/feeling the pulse of the front line – rather than merely sat 'on' it in a detached, dispassionate and disengaged manner.
- *Technocracy* – these *resource holders and policy makers* are expert functionaries covering key activities such as: property and maintenance; finance, legal, audit and IT; marketing, new

product development and supply chain; and HR and talent management.

- *Administration and support* - these *enabling support services* provided by the technocracy are often bundled up into a 'support centre' which interfaces directly with the operational line. The Escalator must ensure that these enabling support personnel are available 24/7 to the front line - especially during weekends and holidays when outlets will experience their heaviest trading periods. Also, the Escalator would do well to put in place operational excellence personnel (experts in operational efficiency and effectiveness) and designated 'flight controllers' who regulate the flow of information/communication/initiatives to the line, sitting between the technocracy and operations.
- *Operational line* - typically seen as *implementers*, the members of this cohort are strategic brand operations leaders, 'interfacing' regional operations leaders and 'local' area managers who manage districts of around 8–30 units (depending on business type and sector).
- *Units and service providers* - these *customer-facing personnel* are the most important link in the chain as the GM, his/her unit management/supervisory team and service providers are the main point of impact with the customer. In short, they are the face of the company. The degree to which the preceding pieces of the jigsaw fit together in order to support this cohort will be a major determinant of customer delight or dismay! Ultimately, the internal service provided to this front-line population (selected on the basis of strong service personalities) will have a major impact on external/customer perceptions of the service.

Inevitably, useful though it is for Escalators in highlighting the core structural components of the brand, this model is fairly normative and descriptive, concentrating on tangible issues of structural alignment/congruence. It does not deal with intangible issues such as competence, power, ideology, politics and culture, all of which are important elements that contribute to either success/failure within food service brands. Inevitably, as the brand gets bigger there will be turf wars amongst functions which the Escalator will have to minimise or eradicate. For instance, whilst strategic leaders and technocrats will have a preference for efficiency ('doing it right'), the operational line (due to its closeness to customers) will lean towards effectiveness ('doing the right thing'). In order to increase effectiveness in fast-growing food service brands, it is highly advisable that the Escalator gets the functions as close to the operational line as possible by 'implanting' marketers and HR in the regional operational line.

- **Robust systems and processes** – effective food service brands leave very little to chance. They are in the business of transforming (in most cases) live, perishable ingredients into quality products served by knowledgeable and enthusiastic staff. Their paramount duty is to ensure the safety and security of their customers – abiding strictly to environmental health, hygiene and safety laws. They also exist to seamlessly and consistently execute their brand promise; consistently seeking to exceed customer perceptions with regards to the core proposition. Key systems and processes that need to be in place to effect these outcomes can be sub-divided into BOH (back of house) and FOH (front of house) systems:
  - **BOH systems** – daily work/task scheduling, daily/hourly audit and compliance checks, food production systems, stocktaking systems and procedures etc.
  - **FOH systems** – daily/hourly standards checks and routines, service delivery system abidance, customer feedback systems etc.

- **Measurement *and* articulation** – many of the systems and processes referred to above will be subject to monitoring, checking and correction/improvement through regular audits (announced and unannounced) by compliance officers or the operational line, coupled with regular operational performance management reviews. But as Chapter 2 intimated, what sets great food service brands apart from the mediocre is a real clarity of purpose amongst *all* their employees. Effective Escalators understand both that 'what gets measured, gets managed' and – more importantly – that 'what gets rewarded, gets done'! They 'get' the importance of measuring, incentivising and ARTICULATING all the way down the organisation to *shift level* (where 'the action must be fractioned'). The KPI Cascade Model below illustrates how Escalators need to set up aligned KPIs that generate intentional and purposeful behaviours at all levels throughout their brand:

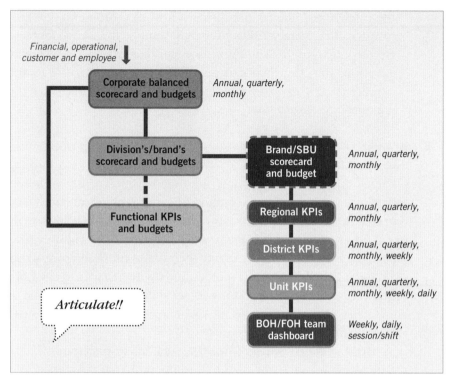

Figure 5 **KPI Cascade Model**

Essentially, the KPI Cascade Model (KPICM) above illustrates how targets/measures flow from the strategic apex to the operational point of impact within food service brands. Escalators must deploy such an approach to ensure alignment, line of sight and coherence of purpose from top to bottom in dispersed multi-site food service operations. Effectively, this model shows a hierarchical cascade of core objectives/targets starting with the top-line balanced scorecard indicators:

- *Corporate balanced scorecard/budget* – these will generally incorporate financial and customer *outputs*, combined with people and operational process *inputs*. These will 'fit' with the top-line brand strategy and objectives.
- *Divisional/brand scorecard/budget* – this will mirror the corporate scorecard, albeit targets will be proportionately adjusted (in multi-brand operations) for the business model (sales, margins, fixed/variable costs), investment plans etc.
- *Functional KPIs/budgets* – these incorporate enabling KPIs which have discreet targets (i.e. supply chain – purchasing

spend variance; marketing – promotional ROI; HR – staff stability/turnover %; property – defect resolution times and 'new build to budget').

- *Operational line* –
  - ○ *Regional KPIs* – financial, customer, operational and people (annual, quarterly and monthly targets)
  - ○ *District KPIs* – same KPIs as region (annual, quarterly, monthly and *weekly* targets)
  - ○ *Unit KPIs* – same KPIs as district (incorporates *daily* targets)
  - ○ *BOH/FOH team dashboards* – unit KPIs broken down into *section, shift* and *session* targets.

Organisational Differentiators

The narrative above outlined the 'qualifying' tasks that Escalators must take during the process of systemising the organisation in order to facilitate its rapid growth – but what do the best do?

- ◘ **Avoid the 'risk paradox'** – one feature of growing organisations is that, as they scale up, fewer decisions are likely to jeopardise the entire future of the enterprise. But paradoxically, more rules and sanctions are introduced at this phase of the life cycle, in order to minimise risk. The Escalator must confront and overcome this conundrum by continuing to allow a degree of flexibility within a fixed frame – a so called 'zone of tolerance' that permits a degree of autonomy and self-expression; that is to say s/he encourages employees to take calculated risks and, at times, 'seek forgiveness rather than permission'. Unless s/he allows these behaviours, the organisation is likely to become hidebound by bureaucratic, ossified behaviours, losing its original spirit of entrepreneurial endeavour.
- ◘ **'The one number that counts'** – very often in food service organisations, KPIs stop at unit level and their execution is hampered by a lack of articulation at team, section, session and shift level. The Escalator must work with his direct team to break down 'macro' monthly/weekly KPIs into 'micro' daily objectives to, first, bring the KPI targets alive and, second, focus on deliverables which will address seemingly detached/distant macro-targets. But what is the one number that really counts in food service at outlet level that everybody can buy into and understand? It is our belief – based on intensive research and practical leadership of growth brands – that NUMBER OF MEALS SOLD is the one number that Escalators should ensure their outlet employees

concentrate upon. Pre-opening staff should prepare quantity and quality; in-session staff should deliver a memorable service experience in order to deliver the one controllable outcome that they should all focus upon as a team, namely: how many meals they produce and serve per session (with minimal returns and comps).

- **Realistic 'stretch targets'** – food service brands might have elaborate KPI cascade and associated incentive mechanisms in place to stimulate the correct behaviours/outcomes but their efforts will count for nothing if the stretch targets themselves are perceived as short termist, unrealistic and unattainable. Indeed, they can have the opposite effect to that intended – destabilising rather than motivating teams to achieve high performance levels. The Escalator must pay careful attention to 'reward and consequence'; that is to say, s/he must resist the tendency to impose (particularly after pressure from investors) stretch budgets and incentivised KPIs that defy all logic. For instance, certain food service concepts – such as full-service gastro dining concepts – require high labour–sales ratios. Applying a slash and burn labour target in such a context (and incentivising people to do so) will have serious medium- and long-term consequences for the brand.

- **Cascaded communications** – the Escalator must explain the 'why' behind all the structural, process and KPI changes in order to achieve buy in – taking the organisation with, rather than dragging it behind them. The earlier s/he puts in structured meetings (in sequence from the top to the bottom of the organisation) with pre-set agendas that address key business challenges/objectives accompanied by instruction/guidance relating to areas of responsibility/accountability/ communication/involvement (so-called RACI – who does what, where, when?) the better! In addition, as the business grows, the appointment of a 'flight controller' who regulates information flows from the functions and the line – to prevent the sharp end of the organisation being overwhelmed by requests and dictats – the more uncluttered the organisation is likely to become/remain. This individual can also act as a sort of internal capacity manager scheduling and synchronising centrally generated key events, promotions, launches and initiatives at outlet level. This will prevent overload and poor execution. Successful Escalators – we suggest – abide by the mantras 'less is more' and KISS ('keep it simple stupid!').

CASE STUDY 8 – **MILLIE'S: SYSTEMISING FOR SCALING UP**
Andrew Emmerson

Andrew Emmerson has led the roll-out and development of some of the food service industry's most successful brands over the course of a 30-year career. Latterly he was an executive director of Domino's Pizza Group and currently holds a number of non-executive positions with a number of high-growth food service concepts.

When you inherit or buy a brand from the original founder, you are presented with a number of issues; not least how you preserve the brand's essence as you attempt to make it more scalable and efficient. Over the years I have been involved in scaling up brands like Dunkin' Donuts in the US, Domino's in the UK and Upper Crust and Millie's Cookies internationally... In all cases I have been involved in driving these brands' next phase of growth; in Millie's case just after the original owner had sold it to the Compass Group (now SSP) in the mid-noughties... At this time we managed to maintain its sales and profit momentum through the 'escalation phase' for a number of reasons:

1. **Cultural continuity** – Millie's was all about 'fresh indulgent treating'... it had been led by a formidably talented husband and wife team who inculcated great values into the brand... they had created a great environment for employees, creating a fun vibe through recognition (regular communications, annual conference, incentives and bonuses; even birthday holiday days off)... this rubbed off externally on customers; they felt good about using Millie's... they could see that the staff were enjoying themselves... I formed an excellent relationship with the founder (he stayed on as a non-executive) and I worked hard with the founding team... keeping the head office in Bury... retaining all the key people... My message was: 'I respect you and I need your help to take this brand to the next stage of growth!'... I personally spent a lot of time out in the stores at peak weekend trading periods – encouraging, complimenting, cheerleading! ...
2. **Incremental change** – I didn't go for any big-bang changes... instead, I focussed on a number of small incremental changes that would add up to quite a lot. ... I asked the team what they thought would improve the business and then harnessed their ideas... For instance, I tweaked the bonus plans to include GP enhancements and wastage reduction; this had a decent impact on the P&L almost immediately...

3. **Leveraging synergies** – as part of a larger portfolio of brands, Millie's could now benefit from greater buying power... Sourcing utilities and product (especially cookies and Coca-Cola) more cheaply put 1–1.5% on the margin immediately... What we ensured was that quality of the main product offer (cookies constituted 60% of sales) wasn't compromised through switching to inferior suppliers etc. ...

4. **Network optimisation** – one of the benefits that Compass could bring was access to sites and capital to invest in more aggressive roll-out... We put on 22 retail and 20 concession stores both domestically and internationally in pretty quick order... In order to 'internally franchise' the store, we tightened up the manuals and specifications... also introducing rigorous operations evaluation procedures (rigorous standards audits)...

5. **Accountability and articulation** – one aspect of the business we consciously preserved was Millie's method of weekly P&L controls... (like Timpson actually) it was based on a 'paper and pencil' recording methodology: store managers had to do their own P&Ls at the end of the week; accounting for sales, labour, cost-of-goods, other overheads, wastage, rent – with a bottom-line profit... The benefits of this were that managers became highly business literate and really tuned into any incentives that were running at any time... They were completely on top of the figures and their weekly and quarterly incentive/bonus progress, and so could communicate immediately to their store teams...

My view is that we successfully transitioned this brand from the founder/creation stage to the escalation stage during the early years of our ownership... I am still on very friendly terms with the founder–entrepreneur now! ... Unfortunately, as time went on and under a succession of leaders, the brand got subsumed into the 'multi-concept' machine and its brand essence was (in my view) radically diluted... At the time, however, I believe we did a good job taking the brand to the next stage...

3.3 Drive Awareness

In addition to accelerating the brand's network and coverage and putting in place a robust organisational infrastructure, which provide solid foundations for growth, the Escalator must exploit new and existing assets by driving customer awareness. The Escalator's role here is to act as a cheerleader, encouraging his/her marketers, agencies and operators to increase the reach and voice of the brand to drive penetration and frequency of visits. In doing so s/he has to seek both to leverage 'push' (brand-driven awareness mechanisms) and to optimise 'pull' (spontaneous customer reaction) strategies. It is important that the Elevator takes both a centrally and locally led approach to extending the brand's customer franchise – simultaneously highlighting the brand's core functional and emotional benefits in the minds of consumers whilst driving traffic through targeted promotions and events.

Awareness Qualifiers

As stated, there are two principle ways that brands can drive customer awareness in order to augment their reputation – by means of what we call 'push' and 'pull' processes:

◘ **Pushing awareness** – here awareness is prompted and carefully orchestrated by the brand by zoning in on *target* customers, feeding them relevant *content* that will stimulate behaviour through appropriate *channels*:

- Understand target customer preferences – the first thing that the Escalator and his team must understand is what their customers want from the brand and how they wish to be interacted with (especially prior to outlet launches). It is worth remembering that it is far more expensive to recruit a customer than retain one, so great efforts must be made to understand core customer preferences. Much of this data will have been gathered during the conception stage of the brand but it is still worth asking a number of pertinent questions, such as:
  - *Core users ('hard-core loyals')* – what is our core demographic? Which group constitutes 20% of guests but 80% of sales/visits? What is their potential lifetime customer value to the brand? What do they seek from the brand? How can we reward their patronage? Which communication media do they prefer? What are the core messages that mobilise them?
  - *Infrequent users ('split loyals')* – what is the secondary demographic in this brand? What are their preferences? Why are they so 'disloyal'? What are their other brands giving them? How can we increase their frequency of visits? What messages do they respond to? How can we mobilise them?
  - *Lapsed ('switchers')/non-users* – why don't they visit? Where can we reach them to sell our message and encourage (re)trial?

- Feed relevant content – the communication from the brand must be distinctive, fulfilling real customer needs, feelings and aspirations. It must always reflect the brand's values and positioning: contra messages will damage its positioning in the minds of existing or potential customers. Relevant questions that can be asked here include:
  - *Brand benefits* – are we emphasising the brand's core benefits? Do we stand out from the crowd both nationally and locally? Are we being sufficiently local in our approach – emphasising our contribution to the local community?
  - *Events/promotions* – are our events and promotions in sync with the brand's positioning? Are they building sustainable traffic and frequency of use or 'giving stuff away' to 'disloyals' and/or 'switchers'?
- Leverage appropriate channels – inevitably brands will directly communicate with customers when they visit the brand. Escalators must also ensure that they are leveraging appropriate 'off-site' channels to prompt awareness and a sense of community. Questions that they can ask with respect to this area include:
  - *Traditional* – what is our exposure through paid (leaflets, radio, regional tv, cinemas, newspapers ads etc.) and free (local newspaper stories/articles etc.) channels?
  - *Contemporary* – what does our website or brand app look like, say and do? Do we have a social media presence (i.e. Facebook, Twitter etc.)? Are we building a community of like-minded raving fans and do they interact with one another? Are we listed in the relevant digital directories? Who is controlling our digital presence; have they got the right skills, motivation and mindset – in short, do they 'get' fast-moving new digital and are they adaptive/responsive enough?

◘ **Pulling awareness** – a more powerful means of generating authentic awareness is driven by customers who pull others into the brand through enthusiastic spontaneous endorsements either through word of mouth or mouse:
  - Word of mouth – here raving advocates recommend the brand to peers, friends and family; these are Fred Reichheld's so called 'net promoters' who – based upon their favourable experiences – passionately sell the brand.
  - Word of mouse – unprompted, unsolicited positive comments

on social media noticeboards, chatrooms, comment boards and discussion sites. These carry a huge degree of influence and weight given their perceived authentic spontaneity. If the brand actually engages with them on these sites – assuming an almost human personality – customer perception of the brand is further strengthened.

Awareness Differentiators

The points above referred to the qualifying tasks that Escalators must supervise and encourage during the process of driving national, regional and local awareness for the brand; but what will make the brand really stand out?

- **Destination of choice** – what Escalators must do is ensure that the brand achieves real cut through to achieve differentiation from the crowd. This is achieved through generating real excitement about and interest in the brand. Often customer choices to visit food service outlets are made on the spur of the moment with little pre-planning. Great brands are opted for first because they have achieved front-of-mind status by having positioned themselves as the place to go ('everybody says how great it is'). Rather than being the default option (i.e. 'everywhere else is full so we'll have to go there'), Escalators should aspire to get people to queue outside their businesses because – contrary to perceived wisdom – queues symbolise success! The fact that people are willing to invest their time deferring gratification in order to experience the brand signals a high degree of loyalty and desire.
- **Touch feelings and aspirations** – many food service brands will tell people about what the brand is rather than what it is all about. That is to say they emphasise functional (product and economic) over emotional (psychological and sociological) benefits. In order to achieve a higher status in consumer minds, the brand MUST touch feelings and aspirations. It must touch the heart not just the mind. Therefore, the content of its messaging and the channels through which it reaches existing and potential customers must go beyond rational argument to high emotional connection. Escalators should ask themselves one fundamental question – why should people **love** this brand? This should then be articulated consistently and relentlessly across all available media.
- **Don't gorge** – one unedifying aspect of the Great Recession – which

had grave consequences for the margins of some large UK casual dining firms – was the use of price discounting (through vouchers) as a blunt instrument to drive traffic. What it did to consumer behaviour was two things. First, it redirected their business to times when the vouchers were valid – not necessarily at the times they wanted to dine. Second, hard-core loyals were upset by the sight of promiscuous switchers brandishing vouchers when they were expected to pay full price. (Indeed, some restaurant managers had to defuse difficult situations by handing out vouchers 'in session' to placate angry diners who didn't have them!) All studies have shown that relying heavily on the price discounting lever ultimately destroys businesses. Escalators must ensure (as the point above argues) that customers visit you for stronger motives than just price!

CASE STUDY 9 – **BYRON: DRIVING AWARENESS**
Tom Byng

Tom Byng is the founder of the acclaimed upmarket casual burger chain Byron which currently has approximately fifty sites. Having established the brand successfully in London, Tom and his team are currently rolling out the brand nationally.

How have we driven awareness of Byron as we have scaled it up? Until 18 months ago we didn't have a marketing department; like most other Originators, I suppose we just did it ourselves at the outset! ... but as the brand has got bigger and moved to areas outside London, we have had to professionalise the whole process... So, really, the act of driving awareness of Byron can be sub-divided into two phases – what have we focused upon during each stage?

1. **Phase One – 'Creation' (0–25 units):** during trial, start up and initial roll-out we concentrated on a few key factors to drive awareness and establish the brand:
   • *Compelling concept* – the first thing we devoted ALL our energies to was creating a compelling concept with **soul** and **personality**; an iconic brand that served American-style fresh burgers 'done well' off a 'small and sweet menu' in individualistic restaurants that all had different, intriguing designs... We sought to provide 'consistently amazing and memorable experiences' so that people would spread the word and keep coming back!

- *Clustering & concentration* – one advantage we had was the benefit of capital investment from a large parent company; this meant that after the proof of concept stages we could launch almost simultaneously in different parts of London... As we opened we created 'local pull' through giant billboard hoardings and 'soft' house-warming launches where we invited locals in to sample our product as a 'thank you' for the disruption we had caused during the build and fit-out process! ...
- *Constant innovation* – whilst we were scaling up the brand, we also kept listening to our customers and teams in the restaurants, and continued to keep fresh and exciting through constant innovation (menu development, 'proper' beer, monthly specials etc.)... this activity signalled to our new and existing customers that we were intent on keeping Byron interesting and relevant...
- *Founder-led PR* – in the early days we spent very little on PR; the PR was mainly me telling the media the 'story' behind Byron... This worked well I think because people like hearing from 'real people' and are more apt to respond to authentic personalities rather than bland corporate speak! ...
- *Social media* – we were also early adopters of the latest trends in social media, taking to Twitter quickly for instance... This generated a very engaged fan base. It was important to me that we remained accessible, normal, that we challenged ourselves to stay fresh... In actual fact, I ran the Twitter account in the early days personally (and probably slightly obsessively!) responding to tweets... I can still be found as a guest editor from time to time...

2. **Phase Two – 'Scaling Up' (25–50+ units):** as we have grown we have certainly not lost our passion for producing fantastic, quality hamburgers delivered by people with personality in highly desirable places; but inevitably we have had to put in a little more infrastructure so that we can continue to 'move the needle' on the existing estate (increasing visit frequency) and launch successfully in areas outside London... Our strategy now is 'to make it as easy as possible for people to enjoy a proper Byron hamburger'... something we have addressed by asking a simple question, 'what do our customers want more of?'... This has meant continuous innovation:
   - *Upgrade website* – recently we have improved our website so that people have a seamless, easy way to find out more about us...
   - *Digitalise payment methods* – as people are getting busier convenience is key – online ordering, mobile payment are all key investments for the business.

- *Broaden range* – we have also thought hard about infrequent, lapsed and non-users... What, if in a party of four, one customer wants a healthier option? They may effectively veto the visit for the whole group... Whilst staying true to our 'short and focused' menu, we recognise the importance of driving perceived choice, introducing well-balanced choices including salads, as well as striving to meet the needs of allergen sufferers...
- *Reward 'loyals'* – the Byron Burger Club has grown from strength to strength and we continue to ramp up the rewards we provide to the more than 90k members of the Byron Burger Club – our most loyal customers... We want to ensure we offer these guys treats or enhanced experiences (such as interesting club events, one-off cook-off nights that enhance our 'burger expert' credibility)...
- *Leverage social media* – in addition to all of this, we now dedicate resources to managing our social-media communities... they are the new and fresh voice of Byron and create stimulating conversations... Indeed, we've had situations where we've been able to solve customer issues immediately, live on Twitter... Having agreed some sensible ground rules, we purposefully picked an avid user of Twitter... We're well placed to express our individuality and respond quickly in 'live' environments... Corporates are often scared stiff of this stuff; but at Byron we understand that, although you can't control social media, you can do a lot to shape a positive message! ... It's my view that the spontaneous feedback we get through social media is a great barometer of how we are doing as a brand: it provides a quick and easy way to get feedback; and because a lot of the rich narrative isn't necessarily directed at us (we are merely 'eavesdropping' on conversations), it has a higher degree of 'realness and authenticity'... What we are working on now is far more robust ways to filter and analyse this valuable big data as a means of continually improving/enhancing our offer...

In conclusion, as you move from creation and through scaling up, it is important, in my view, that the brand leader is there to make sure that the brand personality always shines through... It is my job to grow and stretch the brand whilst preserving its core DNA... ensuring it is consistently articulated throughout the business in whatever we do going forwards...

Final Thoughts

This chapter has considered how brand leaders scale up the concept following its original (successful) creation. It has argued that at this stage of the brand's lifecycle, a process of 'Escalation' is required – a role that must be fulfilled by energetic individuals who have the capacity to act as Escalators, driving a well-ordered rapid push for pre-eminence and category leadership. In scaling up, however, Escalators must maintain the heroic vision and mission established during the previous development phase. To this extent Escalators require both strong leadership and management skill sets; an emotionally intelligent capacity to inspire talent to ever greater achievements, coupled with a rational eye for detail during the establishment of robust systems and routines. Like Originators, the Escalator's style is likely to veer towards dominance, although s/he must combine this attribute with the ability to devolve tasks and decision making, given the widening spans of control caused by the rapid growth of the enterprise. In addition, one of the key jobs of the Escalator is to prevent people becoming overexcited and contain any overconfidence or hubristic tendencies within the expanding organisation. The fact that the brand is rapidly conquering new markets and territories might engender feelings of infallibility, superiority and complacency amongst the more immature members of the brand 'clan'. In order to counter these behaviours, the Escalator must constantly 'bring people back' to the values of the organisation and stress the importance of acting with humility and integrity (recognising that pride comes before a fall).

In the end, though, the Escalator has one virtue that ranks above all others in this crucial stage of the brand's existence: s/he is a fantastic talent spotter who strengthens the organisation by filling key posts with ambitious, motivated, highly capable individuals. Food service businesses are people businesses. The Escalator gets the best people to join him/her on the exciting growth journey! However, at some stage, stellar growth begins to tail off. Now the organisation has to focus less on opening new outlets and more upon 'sweating' the existing estate. The organisation adopts a more stable, less fluid state; it now offers fewer chances of promotion and challenging responsibilities to the talent it has attracted over time. Going forwards, it must focus on evolutionary rather than revolutionary change. The next chapter will consider the next phase of the brand lifecycle which we label 'Evolution'. What does effective brand leadership look and feel like in this phase?

CHAPTER 4 **Evolve**

FOUR

The previous chapter referred to the leadership role of the Escalator during the rapid scaling-up phase of a food service brand's life. But at some point this growth surge peters out in the so-called maturity stage. Why? Well, the brand may have exploited the available vacant space in the market, fast-following competition might have begun to erode its category leading status and/or customers are trading up, down or across the sector! What happens now? The brand can go through a process of bland maturity which transitions into a perish or a revival stage (see subsequent chapters) or it can sustain some degree of growth through a process of *incremental evolution*. At this juncture the leadership requirements of the brand change. The Escalator's primary role to systemise, accelerate and raise external awareness is now replaced by the Evolver's mission to drive incremental change to existing systems and the offer, keeping the brand's positioning compelling, relevant and appealing – without deviating too far from its original core purpose.

Nonetheless, as the excitement and energy of the rapid roll-out stage starts to become a distant memory and the harsh reality of the long hard grind sets in, the Evolver must work hard to adjust skills and mindsets to this new paradigm of incrementalism and continuous improvement. There is a danger during this maturity stage within the lifecycle that – internally – the organisation is beset by bureaucracy and risk-aversion. There might also be a feeling amongst brand members that they are marching to the drumbeat of inevitable decline, given the challenges that they are faced with in the external marketplace. What the Evolver must do now is foster a culture that actively welcomes, embraces and celebrates change. How does s/he do this? We argue in this chapter that effective Evolvers do three fundamental things: first, they maintain a *customer obsession* that will keep them on or ahead of emergent trends; second, they maintain an *agile organisational capability* that can respond and react to new market requirements; and third, they ensure that their organisation has a real *implementation capability* that enables them to land changes seamlessly, quickly and accurately. These will be considered in turn after the case study below, which highlights how one major UK hospitality corporation went about evolving the offer in its wider portfolio through the use of external expert third-party assistance.

CASE STUDY 10 – PREMIUM COUNTRY DINING GROUP: EVOLVING THE PORTFOLIO
Tony Hughes, Paul and Sue Salisbury

In 2000, Mitchells & Butlers (the largest managed pub restaurant group in the UK) made the decision to broaden and evolve its portfolio of offers by introducing a concept that reached a more affluent demographic. Lacking the internal capability to go up the branded hierarchy Tony partnered with successful independent entrepreneurs the Salisburys and Paul Hales (owners of the Lovely Pub Company) to replicate and roll out their Orange Tree pub concept within the M&B portfolio. Their partnership resulted in the Premium Country Dining Group – a softly branded estate of eighty high performing premium destination pub restaurants.

Tony Hughes: We had been extremely successful with our Vintage Inns brand in addressing more affluent needs for *slightly* better upmarket suburban pub restaurant occasions. However, we could see that needs and tastes were changing: wealthy consumers were going up the brand hierarchy and we needed an offer to meet their changing needs, feelings and aspirations. The independent sector had some great operations that attracted customers by being more aspirational; how did we evolve our portfolio, penetrating this lucrative market? Several big multi-brand chains had tried and failed in the past. So we adopted a completely different approach... I had been enormously impressed by the Orange Tree, Chadwick End and had always loved what the Lovely Pubs guys had done in the past... The Orange Tree was blond wood, very modern with a small (but lovely) menu – simple food, beautifully executed; it was also highly successful... But most of all, I could see it was REPLICABLE... it was a simple, clean, crisp operation... However, the most impressive thing was the 'software of the operation' – the people... In restaurants, we are in the entertainment business really; the floor is a theatre – we have a cast, a show etc.! What I loved about the Lovely Pub Company was the quality of their teams and staff and I wanted to bring them on board with their concept not only to replicate the offer but also its culture... In the end, we did a deal with a handshake (no contract) – founded completely on trust – and they helped us replicate the Orange

Tree across our estate (through targeted conversions) in some prime locations... I made sure that the operational team that supported them and the culture that grew up around it was completely ring-fenced from the rest of the organisation... We put in our best senior operator, Kevin Todd, who managed the project and day-to-day relationships with Paul and Sue Salisbury and their partner Paul Hales, acting as a buffer between the organisation and the growing brand... it was an enormously successful partnership that conceived and rolled out a brand which was framed around its guiding bridge statement of 'Stylish Self-Projection'. (It addressed 'new moneyed' consumers who wanted the brand to reflect and reinforce their perceived social standing)...

Sue and Paul Salisbury: In the end we developed nearly eighty pub restaurants in conjunction with M&B under the PCDG banner... but looking back, why do we think it was so successful during its heyday... why did the partnership flourish so well during Tony and Kevin's time?

1. *Compelling concept*: the first thing to say is that the Orange Tree was our fifth development... we had spotted a gap in the market for restaurant food served in a casual way in great pubs with our first development at the Boot at Lapworth; its point of difference at the time being a number of iconic design features (cartoon prints, logs by the door, Ralph Lauren meets Heidi interior design etc.) and great staff who generated a great atmosphere and customer experience (Antipodeans with a great service ethic)... [We are in the business, after all, of SELLING ATMOSPHERE!]... The Orange Tree was a gamble because it was close into the Boot so we built in every point of difference possible to give our customers the opportunity of a different experience... It was also put together with the underlying thought that we might do a softly branded chain; its main influence was a quality restaurant bar with 'an Italian twist'... its points of difference were: an open kitchen, eclectic old/new furniture, mirrors, Italian touches (tins of tomatoes, chopping board, parmesan, wood fired pizzas etc.)... It was simpler and less sophisticated than the Boot but would still appeal to the 'three generations' for every type of occasion...

2. *Trust:* ... The Orange Tree was enormously successful... and while we were thinking about scaling it up, Tony came down with his team and talked to us... He offered us a deal for assisting M&B in a couple of joint developments (a flat rate commission plus 50% of the first year's uplift in profit); an agreement that was honoured and perpetuated until the end of our relationship... What we provided

was the advice on site selection, design, menu development and recruitment/training... The first unit we did with M&B – the Cock at Wishaw – was a direct replica of the Orange Tree...

3. **Performance:** ... The success of our relationship ultimately rested on the fact that what we did together was enormously successful... The Cock exceeded its appraisal by 100%! ... With the exception of a few duds, most openings (we did about 12 per annum) 'shot the lights out'...

4. **Autonomy:** ... But it worked because the company allowed us complete autonomy... We were told by Tony and Kevin to 'treat this money as if it's your own!'... The design process was a pleasure; there were some really good people in M&B – bright people – who brought our vision alive onsite; working with the buildings we'd selected out of the portfolio – rather than just 'force fitting'...

5. **Culture:** ... The most important thing, however, is that we got to pick the people, especially the GM and Head Chef... We also insisted that the kitchen was organised on a brigade system and that there were salaried staff front and back of house for attraction/retention purposes... Also, the fact that the GM was being paid properly meant that s/he could live off-site allowing us (pre-HIMO regulations) to put our Antipodean staff up for free in the vacant space... Thus, we introduced a new culture within a culture within M&B – well-paid, motivated service personalities that were focussed on giving customers great experiences...

6. **Innovation:** ... Our view is that you cannot stand still in this market: people will always steal your ideas. You have to maintain a certain paranoia about continuing to innovate/do things differently to keep one step ahead... Over time we were able to move the concept on – especially in design terms – M&B were actually quite encouraging saying 'do them differently'... They welcomed individuality in this unbranded/soft-branded environment... So we would change drawings and work quite sympathetically with buildings... Again, it meant that anybody who visited more than one of these pubs had a slightly different experience in each one...

Looking back, this was a great team effort but ultimately it worked because of the trusting relationship we built up with Tony and Kevin... it was driven by friendship really... Once they departed and PCDG reached a certain scale, the company started to interfere a little more and the brand ethos was diluted... Nevertheless, we are proud of what we created and established with a large corporate... something that few entrepreneurs have achieved in the past in this sector!

4.1 Customer Insight

The end of the last chapter referred to the need for rapidly expanding food service brands to raise customer awareness so that they are placed front of mind for customers making pre-planned or split-second choices. However, as the market changes and – as in the case of the UK currently – becomes more crowded, brands have to work harder to maintain their point of difference so as to stand apart from burgeoning competition. The challenge is – having established a distinctive position for the brand – how they actively maintain it or passively stand by as it sinks into a miasma of undifferentiated mediocrity!

But how do they sustain their brand's distinctiveness? The start point is that the brand leaders – what we term at this stage 'Evolvers' – foster and encourage an internal obsession with external customer behaviour. Evolvers, rather than focussing purely on internal efficiencies in their quest for growth during the maturity stage, look outwards into the market to establish whether their brand is maintaining a compelling culinary proposition that retains distinctive functional and emotional benefits that address changing customer needs, feelings and aspirations (as our core definition for successful food service brands stated in the introduction). Many Evolvers undoubtedly have access to data that gives them information on competitive trends, relative market share, conversion rates and customer profitability/retention; but rather than just analysing *what* customers are doing, successful Evolvers focus relentlessly on *why* they are behaving in a certain way.

So what are the base-line requirements for maintaining a healthy customer obsession that will enable Evolvers to ensure their brand stays ahead in the market and what makes the best stand out from the crowd?

Insight Qualifiers

So, how do Evolvers keep track of what their current and future/potential customers want from their brand? Essentially, they keep asking for, listening, watching and processing customer information in order to act:

◘ **Ask the right people, the right questions** – in order to establish whether or not the brand is 'hitting the sweet spot' of fulfilling customer needs, feelings and aspirations, Evolvers must ensure that they are not just going through the motions when surveying customer opinion. In the food service industry, brands commonly ask users 'satisfaction questions' relating to food quality, speed of service, propensity to recommend (i.e. NPS) and so forth. But are they necessarily the right questions? Many questions assume brand stasis – they measure the here and now rather than the future. We believe that there is one simple approach that Evolvers can take to help guide where they should *take the brand* by asking customers one simple question: '*what should we stop, start or continue to do to delight you!*' Furthermore, those that are in frequent daily contact with the customers (i.e. GMs and service providers) should be asked: '*if you had the autonomy to change one thing that would improve the customer experience, what would you do?*' In addition, we believe successful Evolvers are notable for not only harvesting information from existing customers and their brand teams but also from other stakeholders that have a valid perspective on the brand's performance/future direction such as suppliers, shareholders and (where applicable) franchisees.

◘ **Listen rather than hear** - asking the right questions to the right people is fine if the brand is willing to listen rather than hear. What do we mean by this? Organisations approaching maturity have been successful in the past by addressing customer needs, feelings and aspirations in a certain way. Why should they change what has proved successful in the past? Often brands – either consciously or unconsciously – become arrogant and complacent; hearing what customers, or their own people close to the customers, are saying about the brand but *not* really listening to and absorbing the feedback to evolve the brand. Evolvers will actively listen to both direct and indirect sources of customer feedback, particularly spontaneous online testimonials.

◘ **Watch actual behaviours** - in addition to asking and listening, Evolvers watch. Why? In spite of what we said above – the requirement for brand leaders to take comments and observations from customers seriously - not everything that customers say can be taken completely at face value. Sometimes the way in which people interact with brands, what they *say* they value and want from the brand, is at odds with the way they actually use (or abuse) it. In some brands, customer competency levels are low (either through poor cognitive skills or unfamiliarity) - people are unable to articulate rationally what they really need or feel - resulting in confusing customer signals. Evolvers must spend time actually observing customer behaviour both within their brand environment and in other contexts (i.e. competitor and corollary brands). This will add emotional context and information to what customers have 'rationally' said.

- **Piece it all together** – once all the available customer information has been gathered together, it must be processed in order to garner key insights. What does it all mean? In truth, unpacking all the data to get to the heart of the matter is both an art and a science. Brands will have data on what customers think of the brand currently and what the market trends are. What Evolvers do is unsentimentally review the information in order to clarify how they move the brand proposition forwards, simultaneously balancing the need to improve/refresh the offer with the requirement to retain its core identity and purpose. Missteps can occur when brand leaders during this stage of the lifecycle force fit what they believe they have heard and seen into a brand re-design that – for self-serving, opportunistic purposes – is cheaper and easier to implement. For sure, conjoining insights with actions is a notoriously difficult process. The ambiguity of what has been said and observed must often be addressed by complex and messy solutions (particularly when the current systems, machinery, processes and people are not fit for purpose!) which brand leaders are loath to implement. Also, deliberate or unintended misinterpretation of the data can actually do more damage to the brand than doing nothing at all – false remedies actually destroying the brand's identity, personality and original raison d'être.

- **Act effectively and efficiently** – once the Evolver has established how the brand should keep moving forwards by establishing what customers want now and in the future, s/he now has to act. This process is dealt with below but, suffice it to say, those brands that stand a better chance of survival and prosperity through the maturity stage have the organisational capability to react to, and satisfy, changing consumer needs quickly. In short, they combine effectiveness (giving the customer what they really want) with efficiency (on time and to specification).

Insight Differentiators

But what sets successful Evolvers apart from the rest during the customer insight process within the maturity phase of the brand lifecycle?

- **Close rather than distant** – successful Evolvers of brands don't sit on the business strangling it to death; they get into the business actively investigating ways to improve it! They are not merely reliant on second- or third-party feedback for their sense of where the business needs to go; they pick up first-hand observation and experience from the front line by being out there. This does not mean that they busy themselves carrying out a series of orchestrated state visits – descending on outlets, acting in a monarchical, detached, flatulent fashion; seeking confirmation from the troops that everything is all right before being driven to the next venue. Successful Evolvers either go back to the floor on a regular basis to touch and take the temperature of employees and customers, or conduct low-key, unannounced visits that are not intended to catch people out but to learn the unalloyed truth about what can be improved to take the brand to the next level.

- **Not everything that is measured counts** – clever Evolvers recognise that not everything in their brand that is being measured and monitors counts. For instance, the brand might have the best customer and market insight systems but do they accurately capture what the totality of brand's existing and potential clientele really think? Customer data systems are good at capturing information on existing users but poor with regards to gathering insights from switchers, lapsed users and non-users. What has driven them off? What keeps them away? Furthermore, there are food service brands in the UK that have respectable NPS scores – indicating that a fair proportion of their customers say that they are very inclined to advocate the brand to colleagues, friends and family – but whose sales remain static. One value-based family brand investigated this phenomenon and found that users were too embarrassed to admit they used the brand and advocate its use (it might affect perceptions of their relative social standing) even though they enjoyed their guilty little secret!

- **Diverge rather than converge** – there is a tendency amongst brand leaders at this stage of the lifecycle to look to other concepts for inspiration. There is nothing wrong with this; at the very least, competitive parity must be maintained. But what successful Evolvers do is try to ensure that their brand continues to be perceived as innovative and fresh. Brands entering maturity can sleepwalk into isometric convergence – mimicking rather than shaping the market.

Partly this stems from a high degree of risk aversion and lack of organisational agility (see below). It is also derived from a paucity of aspiration: an acceptance of mediocrity rather a vision for market-leading excellence.

◘ **Ignore 'cack wizards'** – often brands that are beginning to stall – finding that growth is hard to come by in dynamic market conditions – will turn to consultants and repositioning agencies for inspiration. This can be a useful exercise, providing clarity about the market and how the brand is perceived (i.e. what its consideration levels are amongst various customer groups). It is our belief, however, that brand leaders who – in addition to seeking insight – want cast-iron solutions as to how to move the brand forwards from these sources should beware of this course of action. The marketing industry is notorious for providing marvellous insight but poor solutions to problems. Why? Because every brand has to be viewed in context according to its history, culture, structure and capability. Cack wizards (i.e. clueless 'experts') can do untold damage to a brand by suggesting market remedies that are totally out of context for that brand. Great Evolvers have the cognitive capacity to combine insight into changing customer requirements with their tacit knowledge of the brand and its competitive landscape in order to authorise/instigate incremental changes that will continue its growth trajectory.

CASE STUDY 11 – HOW DO EVOLVERS GENERATE CUSTOMER INSIGHT?
Ian Dunstall

Ian Dunstall is a top-flight brand strategy and development consultant who advises some of the UK's leading hospitality brands. Previously, Ian worked in the UK and internationally as a senior brand executive with some leading-edge hospitality organisations.

Having worked with a number of brand leaders over the past thirty years who have been focussed upon successfully evolving established brands, I would offer the following four insights into their behaviour:

1. **'Dial down' full market research** – the first thing to say might seem counterintuitive... Effective Evolvers of brands don't rely on a lot of full market research to improve their brands incrementally... That

is to say they are people who have a great sense of intuition and self-belief who aren't reliant on guest market intelligence *relating to everything...* They are also quick to understand that you can use market research to *validate* but not necessarily *create...* This is an important insight because *service hospitality is quite unlike FMCG goods...* FMCG marketers recognise that – because of the scale of the upfront investment in new products – they have to carry out meticulous micro-research with both B2B and B2C parties to establish proof of concept before they push the button on design, production, distribution and marketing... In service hospitality, Evolvers can easily set up a trial in a unit and 'go see, touch, feel and hear'... in this sense they can act *quickly* on intuitive hunches garnered from a number of sources rather than voluminous data sets...

2. **Macro-trend awareness** – but that is not to say that Evolvers aren't attuned to macro-economic, technological, social and demographic trends... Corporate Evolvers capture the zeitgeist through watching, listening and harvesting data from a number of channels (print, media, social networks, conferences etc.)... then – within these corporate contexts – Evolvers are adept enough to appoint the right 'exploiters' into the right spaces: people who understand the trends and want to **own** the development of these changing markets... Entrepreneurs are probably more instinctive and, because they have come from the target demographic themselves, intuitively know what is becoming on-trend for their target market...

3. **Understand current guests** – at a practical level, Evolvers tend to get their information and insights through spending far more time in the field than the office... They spend a lot of time on the front line 'touching' their customers and teams... They ask questions and listen intently: *'what do you do with the rest of your leisure time?'* – *'what other restaurant brands do you use?'* – *'why and when do you choose to use us?'* – *'what would you like us to stop, start or continue doing?'* etc. ... Great Evolvers of brands spend a disproportionate amount of time getting into what I call the 'headspace' of their guests... and this can only be fully achieved through face-to-face contact and observation....

4. **Understand wider target market** – but understanding current guests – their changing needs and feelings – in order to evolve the offer to drive visit frequency is (arguably) the easy part... The hardest thing to achieve is – in recognising the changing trends of the market – to broaden the brand's appeal to different customer sets... A lot of brands get locked into what I call 'customer silos';

that is to say, their core customer grouping becomes their only customer set due to the mass migration of their secondary customers into more attractive segments of the market... This has happened a lot in UK hospitality, particularly in brands that once enjoyed a broadly based appeal but have retrenched into servicing their core family market – a situation that has driven 'violent peak' into a small number of dayparts, whilst leaving the rest of the time pretty slack (and hugely unprofitable)... In my view, effective Evolvers are adept at spotting opportunities in dayparts by becoming more democratic; attending to the different needs of customers at specific times and/or ensuring that different customer sets can coalesce (through product laddering, service fit, zoning and environmental management) at the same time...

4.2 Agile Organisation

In order to react to changing circumstances and the need to make incremental changes that maintain its category primacy, the food service brand – during this evolutionary phase – must possess a fair degree of what we term 'organisational agility'. What do we mean by this? All organisational theory points to the fact that companies become more bureaucratic, hierarchical and cumbersome with age. What brand leaders must attempt to ensure is that their organisation is 'loose' rather than 'tight', 'responsive' rather than 'inflexible' and 'nimble' rather than 'inert'. It is highly ironic that when brands are small they try to act big whilst when they are big they try to act small. But how do they do this? This is easier said than done. Instilling or maintaining a small company mentality in a big frame is the avowed intent of many brand leaders during the so-called 'maturity phase'; but often they are defeated in their quest by what they generally claim are invisible counterforces within the organisation. In order for the brand to stay on top of its game, the Evolver must attend to a number of factors that ensure that his/her brand retains the ability to act quickly within the marketplace so as not to get left behind. Again, these can be classified as both qualifying and differentiating elements:

Agility Qualifiers

How do Evolvers ensure their brand remains responsive enough to respond to relentless changes in market requirements?

◻ **Right mindset** - the start point is for Evolvers to exemplify and model a permanent state of change readiness. They signal to the rest of the organisation that stasis is not an option in a rapidly changing market. The way they do this is by imploring their followers to look back at the dynamic history of the organisation, to times when – as the brand was becoming established – heroic figures of the past embraced change enthusiastically. Using symbols, legends, stories and images that relate to exemplar behaviours during the founding and rapid growth period of the brand, the Evolver can invoke the past as a justification for similar behaviour now and in the future.

- ◻ **Ambidextrous structure** – in addition to fostering the right mindset amongst their people – convincing them that the opportunities that lie before the organisation are plentiful and worth pursuing – Evolvers will also pay attention to the structure and shape of the organisation. Sustainable food service concepts are often characterised by ambidexterity; that is to say, they can attend to preserving the core business through the dominant architecture of the organisation whilst prospecting the future through separate, devolved structures. This is something that the scholars O'Reilly and Tushman observed to be a feature of successful organisations in their famous *HBR* article on ambidexterity:

> some companies have actually been quite successful at both exploiting the present and exploring the future, and as we looked more deeply at them we found that they share important characteristics. In particular, they separate their new, exploratory units from their traditional, exploitative ones, allowing for different processes, structures… at the same time, they maintain tight links across units at the senior executive level. In other words, they manage organizational separation through a tightly integrated senior team. We call these kinds of companies 'ambidextrous organizations' and we believe they provide a practical and proven model for forward-looking executives seeking to pioneer radical or disruptive innovations while pursuing incremental gains. A business does not have to escape its past, these cases show, to renew itself for the future…
>
> (O'Reilly and Tushman 2004: 75)

In the case of food service brands, these decoupled units can take the form of separate NPD functions that continually pilot and test new product and service approaches in controlled environments without interference or disruption from the core business. As long as these units are ring fenced against interventions from vested interests and political dominant coalitions within the core, these spin outs can flourish using the resources of the parent. One advantage is that reverse diffusion might take place, where knowledge, ideas and concepts from this new structure permeate back into the main business. Alternatively, food service brands might buy or partner with a firm whose offer, processes and capabilities more effectively fit the new commercial realities and requirements. Although expensive, this approach can be a fast-track route to achieving in months what would otherwise have taken years to effect.

◘ **The 'flexibility within a frame' approach** – in addition to setting up new forward-looking units that are protected from encroachments by the dominant core, Evolvers will try to avoid excessive bureaucracy creep within the organisation by permitting a degree of autonomy through a 'flexibility within a big frame' approach. That is to say, whilst they insist on centrally mandating various fixed policies, procedures and practices (for quality and consistency purposes), they generally allow some flexibility for local autonomous behaviour. They do this for two reasons: first, to build a degree of local responsiveness and agility into their business model at micro-market level; and second, to enrich front-line operators' job roles through providing a certain degree of self-expression. Paradoxically, food service brands that allow a degree of local autonomy actually find that they are able to extract better core control of their operations in exchange. The degree to which operators will be granted flexibility within a frame will be dependent on two principal factors: the Evolver's managerial predisposition (a belief in 'tight' compliance or 'loose' empowerment) and the degree of 'hard', tightly prescribed or 'soft', customised branding.

What Evolvers must guard against, however, is the so-called pendulum effect: often organisations will swing from tight to loose, then back to tight again. Why? Companies are likely to tighten up procedures during challenging commercial conditions (as a form of control, a comfort blanket) or during regime change (to ensure outcome certainty during honeymoon performance periods), then gradually loosen their grip over time as confidence improves; only to revert back to tight if they perceive they are losing control! These pendulum swings are confusing and derailing for front-line operators, who fear coercion and punishment if levels of compliance tighten and are suspicious/mistrusting when a looser approach is granted. Evolvers must also guard against over-exuberance among some of their followers, however, as in some instances some followers will misread the rules of the game, flouting the rules and laws of the organisation to operate semi-autonomously in a deviant manner in order to generate opportunistic growth. This so-called 'added value deviance' is dangerous when exercised by inexperienced or overexcited operators. Evolvers must ensure that their operators seek the explicit or tacit approval of higher authorities before they step outside the fixed framework in order to pursue a locally led growth agenda.

- **Appropriate skill sets** – an organisation that enters an evolutionary phase of its existence, following a sharp acceleration, requires different skill sets and competencies to those required previously. Now the organisation has entered an era of incremental, continuous improvement, the Evolver must ensure that the company has the requisite technical, behavioural and cognitive attributes both to innovate and implement (see below). Many of these skills will have to be imported (see above) and employees that cannot adjust to the new incremental paradigm will have to be replaced. The high-adrenaline atmosphere of fast growth has now been replaced by a more sober atmosphere of continuous betterment. In the Escalation phase of the food service brand, life systems were introduced that must now be patiently improved for operational efficiency purposes. The offer must be continually tweaked and enhanced to stay on trend. Thoughtful, detail-conscious improvers require space next to high-octane operators.

- **Knowledge transfer mechanisms** – within this culture of continuous improvement, the Evolver must pay attention to ensuring that sufficient tacit knowledge exchange is taking place at all levels of the organisation. Generally, lack of knowledge transfer between parties within companies stems from factors such as: lack of trust, scarcity of time, status abuse, lack of absorptive capacity, hoarding and error intolerance. These can be overcome by the Evolver as follows:
    - *Lack of trust* (i.e. a belief amongst innovators that their ideas might be diluted or stolen without reciprocation) – Evolver solutions include face-to-face communications/interaction

(meetings, conferences, store visits etc.); namely, social capital 'face time' that will lead to bonding. Trust and respect can also be built through encouraging operators to work at the Centre and vice versa – this breaks down barriers and false misconceptions (operators often underestimating how hard it is to sell rather than tell).

- *Lack of time* (i.e. distance and BAU activities prevent transmission) – here Evolvers should create time and space for idea exchange. Smarter methods require deployment for instant communication (such as digitally) which will facilitate swifter access to knowledge.
- *Status/power* (i.e. 'time servers' and senior operators refuse to share with newbies) – Evolvers create a set of values that stresses inclusivity, respect and sharing. Make ideas transcend status.
- *Absorptive capacity* – (i.e. personnel don't have the mental capacity to absorb/understand new ideas) – Evolvers encourage the education of those that are willing but 'can't do', and exit those that are unwilling and 'can't do'.
- *Knowledge hoarding* (i.e. innovators jealously guard ideas for reasons of internal competitive advantage) – Evolvers reward/recognise the sellers or purveyors of knowledge and encourage reciprocity between parties through social capital.
- *Error intolerance* (i.e. a belief among innovators that if their ideas fail to work elsewhere they will become coerced into stopping themselves) – remove gameplay, blame, sanction and retribution. Evolvers 'make it ok' to try and fail. They create an environment where people seek forgiveness rather than permission.

Agile Differentiators

But what sets successful Evolvers apart from the rest during the process of ensuring that the organisation remains agile enough to overcome new challenges and threats during the evolutionary phase of its existence?

◨ **Divine dissatisfaction** – the one major characteristic of effective Evolvers of mature organisations is their perpetual paranoia that 'good is not good enough' in the white heat of commercial battle, their abiding restlessness to do things better, smarter and quicker. Their demeanour and disposition signal a state of divine dissatisfaction; that is to say, alert to the dangers of complacency and hubris, they constantly challenge their charges and the organisation to raise their game. As the days of great leaps forward are now over – when compound EBITDA growth was commonly at double (or even triple) digit percentage levels – they must galvanise the organisation to make lots of little strides across a variety of activities and initiatives to keep the brand moving forwards. However, we would counsel against one major enemy: one thing that Evolvers should always be wary about is the ever-present potential of '*internal* menu fatigue' – marketers and operators getting bored with menu items before their customers do! Be constantly challenging and dissatisfied but beware of change for change's sake: don't throw the baby out with the bathwater. Locate the right things to be dissatisfied about.

◘ **Don't cry wolf** – an important point to make, however, is that – at this juncture of the brand's development – Evolvers must be wary of fabricating false crises to use as a call to arms. The reality is that the brand still has a robust business model – people must not feel threatened or become paralysed by unnecessary scaremongering or wholesale changes. The Evolver must keep people on task, relentlessly improving all elements of the brand's marketing mix without being distracted by wave after wave of cliff-hanger rumours.

◘ **Stick to the knitting** – we made the point previously that destructive opportunism (i.e. driving the brand too far away from its mid-point of gravity) is both dangerous and costly. The Evolver is there to refresh and contemporise the brand's core purpose and mission, not to supplant it with something totally different! Evolvers (as we touched on above) must be particularly wary of revolving marketers who wish to make their mark by changing things just for the sake of it (see comments above on internal menu fatigue). In Ansoff's classic terms, Successful Evolvers focus upon: first, sweating their existing assets through market penetration and new customer development strategies; second, product and range expansion; and third, unrelated diversification.

◘ **Quick decisions, sharp meetings** – a simple way to spot whether or not an organisation is lapsing into labyrinthine bureaucracy is through analysing its decision-making patterns and meeting structures/protocols. Bureaucratic organisations have a propensity to impose strict authorisation procedures involving multiple stakeholder sign offs. Decision making is slow and ponderous – sapping the energy of the eager, energetic and ambitious. Additionally, risk-averse bureaucratic organisations provide a flourishing environment for meetings at which the gathered collective consciously hide, avoiding accountability through 'swerving' or deferring important decisions. The Evolver will not tolerate or sanction this behaviour! S/he will lead by example, despatching decisions quickly and holding sharp, purposeful meetings at which people are held to account for their actions and responsibilities (see below).

CASE STUDY 12 – YO! SUSHI: MAINTAINING AGILITY IN EVOLVING ORGANISATIONS
Vanessa Hall, CEO

Vanessa Hall is the CEO of YO! Sushi, the UK's leading Japanese sushi concept, which is currently expanding abroad. Previously, Vanessa has led a number of UK premium brands, such as YO! Sushi, All Bar One, Premium Country Dining Group and Browns, through major evolutionary transition and international expansion. Vanessa has been involved in hospitality brands for over 20 years both in financial and operational leadership roles, and at different stages of the brands' lifecycles.

When brands have transitioned through their exciting creation and rapid roll-out phases to reach a decent scale, the brand leader is faced with a number of challenges. First, as they get bigger, brands tend to become less nimble and more cumbersome; decision making becomes more protracted… Second, brand members who have experienced the rush of the transformational early days have to adjust to a new paradigm, that of incremental improvement in order to patiently and steadily move them forwards. The question is how does the brand leader at this stage propagate a sense of optimistic momentum, urgency and energy? Based on extensive experience evolving brands, I would point to a number of things that successful Evolvers do in order to take the game forwards:

1. **Pace and urgency** – the first thing an Evolver must do is keep up the levels of pace and urgency within the organisation. Given the dynamic nature of business – and particularly due to the intensive competitive context of UK casual dining at present – a small company mentality is still needed – flexible, quick and nimble, forward looking. Weekly flash meetings with the team are a great

way to drive action... short blasts of communication and updates that are immediately cascaded... keeping people up to speed on developments, tracking the progress of key initiatives etc. ... this sets the dynamic tone for the organisation...

2. **Blended team** – what you need in evolving brands is to be able to harness and benefit from a blended mixture of experience, skills and personalities – founders and brand members who have been on the journey since day one need complementing with newbies who bring different perspectives and insights... It is the challenge of the Evolver to blend these groups together in order to ensure that 1+1=3! ... The danger is that the old guard who were part of the original heroic mission of the brand rely on history, 'the way we did things in the past', and the newbies immaturely challenge every aspect of the 'way things are done around here'... If the Evolver can drive the skills and values from both old and new to work together constructively, forging mutual respect in order to craft a refreshing/sustainable trajectory for the brand... what a great competitive edge that would be.

3. **Supporting values** – underpinning the company and in order to deliver the blended team mentioned above... you need a guiding compass for behaviours that keeps people on message and on track... common values... intended to create and drive intentional and purposeful behaviours... These should be woven into communications and KPIs to reinforce and shape actions... Evolving organisations need this glue so that brand members do not forget what the brand is all about! ...

4. **Efficiency AND creativity** – perhaps one of the greatest challenges for evolving brands is the tension that will exist between the need for systematic efficiency juxtaposed against the requirement to stretch the concept through creative innovation in order to keep on trend... In short, the organisation must learn to 'walk and chew gum'... Obsessing about efficiency at the expense of creativity leads to compliance, atrophy and decline... Over-indexing on creativity at the expense of business discipline leads to chaos, disorganisation and bleeding... The Evolver must veer away from binary either/or solutions... S/he must insist that that brand members simultaneously attend to both vital processes without compromising either...

5. **Less is more** – in order to achieve both efficiency and creativity it is the job of the Evolver to provide FOCUS... What I mean by this is that in an attempt to outpace the market, see off the competition and deal with external distractions, there is a tendency to try to do too much... It is the job of the Evolver to distil the 'must dos' and

jettison the 'nice to haves'… S/he must bring clarity and precision (through task, structure and organisation), along with the sense of urgency I talked about above…

Being an Evolver of a brand is a testing job, requiring a balance of both organisational and creative skills… I would end by saying that it is crucial that the Evolver ensures that their brand never slumps into a business-as-usual mentality… S/he must constantly reinforce the fact that incremental change is a necessity if the brand is to stay ahead… But s/he must also attend to the nuts and bolts of daily delivery… The days of stellar start-up growth may be over but there is a huge prize to be gained by, first, doing it better and, second, stretching the concept to engage new customer groups and markets…

4.3 Implementation Capability

Implementation capability is the essential handmaiden of organisational agility! While it is necessary for evolving organisations to retain a high degree of responsiveness and flexibility in the face of a fast-moving market, it is their ability to execute change quickly which separates the men from the boys. This is not easy. Often many changes are required simultaneously and in rapid succession. Also, a change in one system or process can have a knock-on effect elsewhere. Efficiency initiatives that involve simplifying workflows and practices can have unintended effects in other areas: for instance, improvements to labour scheduling and rostering can derail service excellence (because they bring with them prohibitive new rules and restrictions). Effectiveness programmes, like design changes intended to improve the customer experience, can be undermined by poor execution and a lack of resources. Having cracked customer insight and set up an agile organisation, the Evolver must ensure that s/he can quickly translate strategic policy into action, paying due regard not only to the *what* and the *why*, but also to the *how*. In manufacturing organisations where managers can incubate, test and evolve initiatives in a single-site environment, implementing change can be supervised and scrutinised closely. In food service brands – characterised by distance, perishability and heterogeneity (see Introduction) – the process of landing change is particularly challenging. It is further complicated in inter-company retail formats such as franchising where one party (the franchisee) refuses to cooperate with the other party (the franchisor), shirking their responsibility to implement changes that they regard as unnecessary and (most commonly) too expensive. So how do Evolvers ensure that any incremental changes they promulgate and support cut through, even in benign agile contexts?

Implementation Qualifiers

The base-line qualifiers that Evolvers need to focus upon in order to ensure seamless implementation are as follows:

- ◪ **Top-team alignment** – the start point for great implementation within brands is the top of organisation. Evolvers should ask themselves whether or not collective decisions made at executive level are really bought into by the whole team. Are executives agreeing to various projects and initiatives, then paying lip service to them when it comes to implementation? Are turf wars between functions and operations hampering execution? Great food service brands are bound by common purpose – especially at the top tier of the organisation. If factions or fractions develop at this level they will be mimicked at more junior levels within the brand. Half-hearted commitment to various changes (for political, opportunistic or expedient reasons) will undoubtedly lead to dilution and inconsistent delivery. The Evolver must really ensure that his/her top team really buys into the fact that, once its members agree to do something, they must all go away and make it happen – quickly!

- ◪ **Operational input** – often the operational line will complain that changes in practices and policies have been imposed upon them with scant communication or without input from those that will be most affected by the changes (i.e. front-line service providers). Sometimes they are correct: overenthusiastic functionaries with a poor understanding of the reality of front-line operations will devise schemes that are doomed to fail. On other occasions, the line is engaging in a heightened form of game play. Under great pressure to perform, they deliberately absent themselves from discussions regarding the content and timetabling of new initiatives, in order to divert attention from their (mediocre) performance by claiming that they have been ignored or bypassed during the process. The Evolver has to be wise to these games, ensuring operations are fully involved in, and consulted about, important changes that might have serious ramifications for customers if they go wrong. S/he must also have the guile and nous to sense when operations are seeking to pass the buck on issues about which they clearly avoided volunteering any help or guidance.

◘ **Gates and filtration processes** – in addition to ensuring that the operational implementers are fully involved in crafting business-critical initiatives, Evolvers will ensure that their brand has checks and balances in place sifting the quality and quantity of information that flows from the centre to the units. This will usually entail operational services managers (OSMs) – 'flight controllers' – overseeing ERP systems (with a calendar of events and releases), orchestrating and regulating the flow of initiatives and new policies to the units. In ideal circumstances, OSMs work closely with decision makers in the line to decide whether or not specific information releases or initiatives are commensurate with operational priorities, preventing the onward transmission of non-value-added instructions. Evolvers are conscious that the line needs to get on with the day job as well as landing initiatives: they will free up capacity for the line by restricting information releases and downloads to certain times of the day (usually pre-opening) or week (typically Friday), in order to prevent their GMs from being distracted by a constant barrage of data.

◘ **Feedback and reset mechanisms** – not all initiatives will be fit for purpose at the first attempt. Evolvers will ensure that feedback loops (such as digital hotlines) are in place from the line to the centre providing real-time intelligence on the impact and success of certain initiatives (such as menu launches and new promotional mechanics). The Evolver will also hold regular feedback meetings between operators and senior managers, considering a range of issues such as which product lines work, which practice changes are required and what operational improvements can be made to increase efficiency and effectiveness. In addition, Evolvers will make great efforts to cull legacy practices and systems that have lost their relevance. Organisations are notoriously bad at reviewing and reducing redundant reportage, red tape and ossified operational instructions. Evolvers will make regular efforts to reset their operations following regular reviews of all their practices and procedures. In order to do so, they will pose the question: what is mandatory for legal and operational excellence and what is superfluous or nice to have?

Implementation Differentiators

But what sets successful Evolvers apart from the rest, allowing them to ensure that their organisations have the capacity and capability to drive through value-added incremental change seamlessly and effectively?

- **Executional pride** – the successful Evolver is someone who engenders a 'right first time' mentality within his/her brand. S/he is also able to convince her/his charges that crushing costs that don't affect the customer experience – to achieve a 'least' rather than 'lowest' cost operational paradigm – is a noble cause that can unlock funds for other worthwhile activities. Also, functions are encouraged to get close to the operators, and vice versa, to minimise misunderstandings and missteps. Brand members celebrate and exult executional excellence, behaviourally conforming to Henry Ford's dictum 'quality means doing it right when no one is looking'. Evolvers have to drive a lot of incremental change to maintain the brand's momentum; ensuring implementation, execution and delivery meet the highest standards is absolutely key to the brand's sustained progression.

- **Wider stakeholder buy in** – in addition to co-opting the organisation in their mission to professionally discharge initiatives and core objectives, the Evolver will also pay heed to the need to get third-party stakeholders to buy into the company ethos. Vital enablers such as contractors, suppliers and service providers must understand that the brand has a certain expectations regarding quality, speed and responsiveness. Successful Evolvers will work hard to ensure that these third parties are made to feel like partners in the journey to build and sustain the brand's pre-eminence. They achieve this through communication (i.e. supplier conferences) and by insisting upon fair and equitable contractual practices/treatment being meted out by the company.

- **Project-management skills** – as the organisation has grown, leadership and middle management have concentrated on rolling out the original concept. Now that they are in the process of evolving it across a (potentially) large estate, they will require some personnel with good project-management skills. In the past, the need for these skills might have been shunned because they were regarded as too 'scientific' and 'over rational'. The size of the enterprise and requirement for relentless incrementalism, however, now means that people with good planning and organisational skills need to conjoin with the 'emotionals' to get things done on time and to specification. A blended set of skills is now required by the organisation and successful Evolvers will work hard to ensure that organisation has the right balance in order to move forwards.

CASE STUDY 13 – **DOMINO'S PIZZA: IMPROVING OPERATIONAL IMPLEMENTATION**

Patricia Thomas

Patricia Thomas is an industry-leading franchise consultant, having previously been Director of International Development and Executive Director of Operations of Domino's Pizza Group (DPG) UK. Previously, she held senior positions with Domino's (US) following stints at the Michel's Baguette French Bakery Café franchise and Houlihan's Restaurants.

When I joined DPG UK as Executive Operations Director in 2006, I identified two major objectives: to transform the *quality* and the *speed* of operational execution in our store network. Due to the growth surge of the brand, it was acknowledged that our operational team had fallen behind in ensuring that the basics were done brilliantly – certainly our franchisees lacked a degree of faith and buy-in to what they were trying to achieve... Standards and systems adherence were perceived by some as unnecessary effort and cost... Lip service was paid to enforcing standards and OM breaches were not uncommon. However, the one major attribute that DPG had was a fantastic culture that had been fostered by the CEO and his team – a healthy paranoia about keeping ahead of the competition... a hunger and real desire to anticipate or fix chinks in the armour that might prove costly in market-share terms in the long run... This applied particularly to network growth, product development and marketing... But how did I galvanise our operations team and franchisees to transform quality and speed at the store level? ... when I reflect back, it was through creating *strong relationships* and a strong sense of *mutual self-interest* (what was good for us as a franchisor was also good for them as a franchisee)... This is how I went about it...

Coming into the role, I decided that I would spend the first 100 days visiting 100 stores to watch and listen... this period allowed me to acquaint myself with the operations team who accompanied me to their stores and to 'touch' over 50 of the 150 franchisees we had at that time... This was in addition to the day job – administrative duties, meetings, budgets, staffing, marketing and so on didn't stop for me to do this! ... It became clear to me that the operations team required redirecting and that our franchisees needed to understand why operational excellence was important to their bottom line... I started to work on our relationships with our franchisees by having informal meals and drinks with many of them, bringing them back into balance (overcoming objections and problem raising) by asking about *how* they had got here today – listening to their stories, which almost served as a conscious reminder to them *why* what they were doing was important... We also set up regular calendar communications events which were designed to inform franchisees directly what we were doing, seeking their buy-in to changes... The message that I relentlessly conveyed during these interactions was that we had to get better at executing the brand... I used my experiences in the US as a powerful anecdote to highlight how operations that lose focus on product quality and speed of delivery can drift off... but what I also did was to empirically demonstrate a financial link between investing in staff training, deployment and equipment, their positive effects upon operational execution and customer satisfaction/sales out-turns. I used live examples of operators that had good operational evaluation reviews (OERs) and speed of delivery scores that had translated great sales figures (this had never been done before)... showing that investing in your business really pays off! To ensure constancy of purpose we also tied OERs and delivery times into specific targets with related rewards and consequences... At the same time, the company introduced real-time comparative (store vs store) delivery data that showed up on FOH EPoS systems at store level and invested heavily in digital ordering systems... the cost of which was shared between the company and the franchisees...

The net impact of all these changes was a dramatic improvement in operational execution... OER scores moved from 3.53 stars on a 5-star scale to 4.27 stars – the highest achievement of any market in the Domino's system. During this period of time, average sales per unit grew by 47% and the number of stores in the UK and Ireland grew by 62%... but – as I said – the way we drove these changes was by fundamentally improving our relationships with our franchisees; not through formal committees (where members can sometimes be driving their own agendas) – but by one-to-one, face-to-face communications where we got the message over... reminding franchisees about the 'why', selling the financial benefits of 'doing it right' and providing extra data/support to make it happen... One further thought I would add is that given the transitory nature of much franchisor management, it is important that operational transformation is led by leaders with credibility who really *monitor and care about franchisee profit*... winning franchisors make good, sustainable profit rather than bad, short-termist gains! ...

Further Thoughts

This chapter has considered how leaders evolve food service brands when they reach the 'mature' stage of their existence. During this phase, their principal task is to keep the brand relevant, vibrant and fresh by making targeted incremental changes; honing its emotional and functional distinctiveness whilst maintaining its core purpose and mission. The way in which so-called Evolvers do this is to: first, harvest accurate *customer insight* that informs the changes they need to make; second, engender a high degree of *organisational agility* to absorb change; and third, construct capacity to *implement*, deliver and execute changes. Evolvers have a tough job. The organisation is on a slower growth curve than it was during its 'escalation' phase when a great deal of pioneering excitement was felt by brand members. Now they are confronted with the prospect of making small, hard-fought gains in order to sustain progress, it is the task of the Evolver to generate emotional buy-in to their superordinate vision to honour its founding fathers by sustaining and advancing its pre-eminence. What leadership style do they adopt in order to achieve this?

Unlike the origination and escalation phases, during which a dominant leadership style was required to bring the heroic mission alive through respectively creating and then rolling out the brand, Evolvers need to take a more participative approach. The organisation is too large and complex for Evolvers to take all of the key decisions; they are better served by devolving responsibility to people who are closer to the customer. A major by-product of this involving, delegative approach is that brand members feel a greater sense of autonomy and personal contribution; emotions that are likely to result in high levels of engagement and commitment.

Unfortunately, organisations that morph into highly risk averse, bureaucratic entities during the maturity stage elicit opposite feelings amongst their people. Here employees are prone – due to high levels of control, compliance and surveillance – to feel detached and disengaged. It is at this point that the organisation stands a very high chance of disappearing from the competitive landscape. In short, they perish. It is to this stage of the brand lifecycle that this book will now turn its attention.

CHAPTER 5 **Perish**

FIVE

The previous chapter discussed how, once food service brands reach a certain degree of maturity, their survival and prosperity becomes highly contingent upon the active evolution of their marketing mix to address changing customer needs. But what happens if brand leaders neglect this task, whether through incompetence, lack of resources or the sheer obsolescence of their product? In short, the brand will perish! Often, the demise is not instant – it's usually a drawn out and protracted affair, during which successive leadership regimes are unable to stem the spiral of doom. Once brands are locked into a process of decline, brand members – some of whom have been on board since its inception – begin to experience feelings of disillusionment, helplessness and anxiety. The most talented move on, leaving the mediocre behind to deal (badly) with the task of trying to reverse the brand's downwards trajectory. In some instances (see the next chapter), the brand can be revived in the nick of time by transformational leaders who take radical and decisive action, restoring the brand's reputation and trust with both customers and employees. Most, however, are beyond retrieval. They have a rapidly diminishing franchise that offers few distinctive benefits to either employee or customer constituencies. In order to avoid being labelled as pariahs (and suffering the costs of failure, affecting their long-term employment prospects within the industry), sensible brand leaders will, at this stage, attempt to disband the brand in an orderly fashion. Depending on the views of the asset owners, they will try to salvage some value for shareholders from the wreckage by managing the exit: by going into 'pre-pack' administration (or 'Chapter 11' in the US) to protect viable assets from creditors, closing uneconomic sites and selling off anything of tangible value (such as trademarks, sites etc.).

But why do food service brands die? Why do those that were once vaunted, feted and celebrated as category-leading champions disappear completely from the radar? We think this is an important question because, first, most books on branding offer few observations on the symptoms of terminal decline and, second, it would be helpful for our readers – in addition to absorbing the lessons of success – to understand the origins of extinction. Sometimes we can learn more by examining apocryphal stories of failure than de-sanitised stories of victory! In our view, brands fail for three principal reasons (some which are interconnected). First, they have incompetent management, lacking in judgement, common sense and tacit expertise, that leads them down the path of destruction. Second, some brands are – for a whole host of reasons – starved of the financial and human resources required to renew and refresh their infrastructure and proposition. Third, brands become become obsolescent – irrelevant, outmoded and unloved. These will be considered in turn after the case study, below – which serves as a cautionary tale to over-exuberant UK food service leaders at the present time!

CASE STUDY 14 – **WHY BRANDS PERISH IN THE US**
Frank Steed

Frank Steed has had a long and illustrious career in the US food service industry, building and leading some of the sector's most successful brands over the past thirty years. He now runs his own consultancy advising owners and leaders on brand development (particularly within the franchising domain).

Why do Brands perish? … A good question! … The US is far more mature than the UK market – we have had over fifty years launching and developing food service brands; inevitably there have been some notable failures… In my view, there are three main reasons why [once successful] US food service brands have failed…

1. **Convergence** – the biggest reason, in my view, why US food service brands have failed – particularly within the 'sit down' casual sector – is because they merged… that is to say, they all began to look and feel the same over time… The fast casual sector that has emerged over the past fifteen years, offering quicker, less expensive ways for consumers to get food, made full-service casual theme brands look outdated and irrelevant; places where the menus looked the same, the service was average and the environments unexciting… Brands in this segment of the market did not evolve… they did not work hard enough at setting themselves apart… there was no sense of differentiation or uniqueness…

2. **Transitional failure** – in the wider market, where there is a rich history of start-ups by entrepreneurs in the US – probably more so than in the UK where many brands have been 'founded' by corporates – many brands have experienced severe transitioning issues... What I mean by this is that egoist founders hang around far too long, eventually strangling their own creation through inadequate planning and evolution... They have remained stuck in the past and been change averse... Fresher leadership approaches and new perspectives were required to drive the brand towards its next stage of development but these founder egoists have hung around for too long causing (terminal) damage to what was once an extremely promising concept...

3. **Short-termism** – in the US market, it almost seems at times as if the VCs [venture capital funds] are buying up everything... The issue is that they have short-term goals which are often at odds – particularly in franchised environments – with the long-term health of the brand... They often apply immense pressure on talented management to 'produce' against exacting ROI and profit-growth goals... Their actions have (in some cases) led them to blow up some really great brands through so-called 'value engineering' or 'cost-minimisation' strategies designed to extract cash and (temporarily) inflate profit, allowing them to spin the asset on after a few rapacious years of ownership... In some instances, VCs have done a sterling job but, all too often, they have starved promising brands of the necessary oxygen to grow and prosper over the longer term through excessively short-termist financial, rather than industrial, strategies...

5.1 Incompetent Leadership

The main reason (previously successful) food service brands fail is simple: incompetent brand leaders squander their inheritance through arbitrary decision making or wilful neglect. They might have been promoted into positions of authority beyond their level of capability or fallen victim – due to their position of absolute power within the organisation – to gross levels of hubris and narcissism. They are incapable of seeking advice or taking on board wise counsel. Often they display extremely short-term behaviours, acting either as hired guns or in a totally self-interested manner. Sometimes they disguise their true agenda behind a cloak of rhetoric, but their behaviours betray their true intent. They are not interested in building legacy or acting as stalwart stewards or guardians of the brand; they are purely focussed upon acting as agents of capital. But what do we regard as the common typologies amongst this crucible of failure? And having fallen victim to incompetents, how can companies remedy the situation?

Common Typologies

Based on over seventy years of experience in this industry, we believe that there are four leadership types who blow up food service brands, each with its distinctive characteristics:

- **The clueless** – this type of leader is either completely unsuited to running a food service brand or lacks the skills to manage a brand during its transitional phase of development. With regards to a lack of tacit expertise of the industry, it is not uncommon for brand owners – in order to seek new perspectives – to go outside the sector to hire new leaders; in spite of all the evidence (both practitioner and academic) that promoting talent from within or across the sector from similar concepts is the most fool-proof way of safeguarding a brand's future. Sometimes hires have been made from food retail, for instance, but these new recruits – steeped in knowledge of functional retail – lack a recognition of the centrality of service performance, on-site production and emotional connectivity within a hospitality context. Tangible factors such as range, availability, quality and price are the main drivers of customer satisfaction in food retail. Intangible attributes such as service, sociability and environment are just as important within food service. Also, leaders from a food retailing background – where brands are highly systemised and homogenised – often cannot cope with the heterogeneous nature of food service; they are insufficiently attuned to the fact that one size cannot fit all within this context (see Introduction). Lacking these insights, the clueless leader wrecks the emotional dynamic of the brand by searching for solutions based more upon efficiency than effectiveness. With regards to the wrong leader being in place at the wrong stage of the brand's lifecycle, the point was made earlier that each role during the various transitions must be matched by appropriate leadership skills. Whilst it is possible in some instances for some leaders to fulfil multiple roles, the likelihood is that owners of decaying brands negligently persevere with the wrong leaders, who have the wrong skills at the wrong time in the brand's development, resulting in dire consequences for all concerned (such as employees, customers, shareholders, suppliers and communities).

- **The reckless** – this category of leader jeopardises the future of the enterprise by making high-risk decisions in an effort to achieve preposterously stellar growth and/or generate dubious shareholder value creation. Unsuitable assets are acquired for the sake of the appearance of scale (the notion of expansion being conflated with growth) or complicated exercises in 'value engineering' are conducted. The reputation of the brand is diminished rapidly by vainglorious financial, rather than industrial, strategies that end in unmitigated disaster. It is not that the leader in this instance is clueless; rather they possess a dangerous combination of a lack of self-control and a low boredom threshold. They seek immortality by putting all their chips on red; and in some instances, they get away with it on the first or second occasion. Inevitably, however, they get found out. To the reckless, taking risks is a form of aphrodisiac – it is a stimulant that they crave in order feel energised, excited and alive. But why are these chancers in a position of authority in the first place? Likely explanations include brand-owner greed (the fact that they buy into the wrecker's vision for their own self-serving financial purposes), executives dangerously morphing into this category through boredom (they have been in position too long) and executives who are subject to a complete lack of corporate governance (checks and balances that thoroughly review key strategic decisions). Whatever the reasons, this type of leader comes with a strong health warning: they should either not be appointed in the first place or stopped in their tracks before they do irreparable damage!

- **The egoist** – the egoist is probably one of the most common leader types connected to failing food service brands. This individual has an almost improbable and delusional sense of infallibility. Their lack of self-awareness coupled with a misguided belief in their divine superiority drives them to make decisions without consulting others, whose views and opinions they regard as derisory or unworthy. Soon, the egoist has created an organisation which relies upon them for all the answers; decisions are deferred or delayed for fear of retribution or being cast out of the circle of patronage. The all-powerful monarch, with a sense of unbridled self-destiny, has surrounded him-/herself with compliant followers who have learnt to flatter and preen the leader's sensitive ego rather than draw their attention to unpalatable truths. But because the egoist is in it for themselves rather for the long-term prosperity of the brand (the project is about them rather than the common good), the brand is usually doomed to failure. Following conception, no successful brand can be the preserve of one man or woman. Engagement and innovation can only be sustained through a feeling of common purpose and public recognition of the contribution of others. The egoist cannot see or recognise this. Eventually, even though surrounded by sycophants, they are left isolated and become detached from the truth. At some point, a regime change will occur and all those that the egoist believed were close colleagues and confidents will spurn and ignore them.

- ◘ **The toxics** - our final category of failing brand leaders (although not totally mutually exclusive to the types outlined above) incorporates the consciously venal! These sociopaths have managed their careers successfully because they have been outstanding at managing upwards. Unlike unselfconscious egoists, they nastily plot, scheme and dissemble deliberately to get their own way, whatever the human consequences. Lacking any empathy for the feelings of others, they actively seek to divide and rule - deliberately setting brand members up against one another through gossip and misinformation. They do this because they believe that it augments and strengthens their position: they become indispensable puppet masters - the only people who can lay claim to being able to control the unruly rabble (which they themselves have created). Toxics are hard to catch and despatch because they are sly and mendacious. As they are used to preying on the insecurities and fears of others to control them, they are artful in seeing off any challengers by deploying equally ruthless tactics (i.e. whispering campaigns challenging their moral probity and good character). But in the end, their gameplay hangs them with their own rope. Toxics run out of people, the brand runs out of energy and they run out of track. At some point, their tactic of blaming everybody else for poor performance loses credibility and they become the victim - along with the brand, which is probably too far gone for redemption.

Remedies

Undoubtedly, the typologies above make sober reading for those charged with the responsibility of appointing and monitoring effective brand leaders. Leaders who fit one (or all!) of the categories listed above are likely to inflict lasting damage to the brand at any point during its cycle. How can this be avoided?

◻ **Matching** – the first thing that all boards and shareholders need to do is unsentimentally establish what the leadership requirements of their brand are (i.e. what stage of the brand lifecycle they are in) and match the leader type accordingly. But as this section shows, selection should be made not only according to technical capability; it must also involve behavioural and cognitive assessment. Along with questions relating to experience and tacit knowledge of the sector, when confronted by credible incumbents and candidates, appointers should ask:

- Does this person have the appropriate skill set to transition this brand through its current stage of development (i.e. escalate, evolve or revive)?
- What is the *authentic* leadership style of this individual? Would I like to be led by him/her? What do people that have been led by this person in the past say about him/her?
- Will this person leave a legacy that positively strengthens this brand?

◻ **Regular and rigorous assessment** – once brand owners are sure that they have got the right person in place, they should regularly monitor the incumbent's performance. This seems a trite and obvious statement but it is rarely done well! Why? Often brand owners (shareholders and boards) begin to suffer from Stockholm Syndrome – they get too close to their CEO 'captor'. They take what they are being told at face value because they become too emotionally involved with the individual concerned or they believe that the brand leader's exit would reflect badly upon themselves (especially if they appointed him/her in the first place!). Often, the Chairman–CEO appraisal involves a cursory chat rather than an in-depth assessment of performance. A brand can drift into oblivion because the monitor of the brand leader is asleep at the wheel, accepting crapulous excuses for poor performance, whilst the very architect of the brand's demise sits in front of him!

◻ **Decisive action** – owners, shareholders and boards can react too late to senior 'misleadership' within a brand. This failure to grasp the nettle sooner rather than later can result in dire consequences. For instance, having an incremental evolver in place when a transformational reviver (or vice versa) is needed can hasten the brand's extinction. Competent brand owners should take a view of where the brand is now and where it needs to be and dispassionately assess whether the leadership they have in place can get them there. If yes – all well and good. If not – incumbents should be offered generous terms to exit the business quickly and with good grace.

CASE STUDY 15 – **TALES OF INCOMPETENT BRAND LEADERS**
Chris Edger

The following reflections on incompetent leader types are based upon both our own observations and the reminiscences of others interviewed for this book.

The clueless – 'So then this "big chain" guy walked in to run our smashing little multi-brand collection of sites that needed nurturing and developing... He was totally out of his depth... we realised that "although he had a big hat, he had no cattle!"... He was full of bullshit... He convinced the board to pour money into initiatives and systems that were designed to increase efficiency and control... He had no clue about customers – none whatsoever about scaling up and evolving brands... In fact, when I reflect back, we should have spotted the fact that the brands he'd initiated or supervised in his previous "big role" had either struggled, limped on or died... "#Bullshit Barry" we called him... Utterly useless... Irony is, he's gone on to bigger and better things after he finished us off!'

The reckless – 'There was this great little concept based around [   ] cuisine that really excited customers – truly capturing the spirit of the times... A television series and book that were out at the time really stoked up interest and passion for this type of concept. The two guys that founded the concept were passionate foodies... The problem was that as they scaled the brand up through a franchise system, franchisees found that really they were buying a menu with very little else... [The founders] were totally reckless with regards to (not) providing a proper blueprint for the brand... There were no systems and processes... the whole thing ended in disaster really because of an inattention to BOH detail... It could have been a great brand – and for a while it really did well... but you can't found a food service franchise brand on just a menu and a fascia... They tried to sprint before they could walk, with dire consequences for a lot of the good, hardworking people they signed up!'

The egoist – 'Two guys founded this brand and it had real early momentum – one did the food and operations and the other did the deals... Problem was the guy who really had a handle on how the operation worked got fed up with his partner and left, having been bought out by his partner after a few years... The hilarious thing was the "deals guy" then thought he could run the operation! ... Suddenly he became an expert in [   ] cuisine and food service operations... and when the company ran into cash-flow issues and was refinanced by private equity, he was still kept on (with a reduced shareholding) because the new owners – who had made a mistake of getting rid of a founder–entrepreneur in a business they'd owned in the past – kept him on because they believed he was the guardian of the DNA! ... The architect of disaster more like! ... By the time they realised what an idiot he was – he made all the decisions himself and lost all the key people... the brand had already been superseded by other start-ups that had stolen its clothes and done the concept better; its point of difference had disappeared and the brand was on skid row...'

The toxic – 'I remember that at that time in the organisation, we set up separate grill and carvery concepts that were overseen by one individual – let's call him Bruce. Bruce was under a lot of pressure because the assets we converted into these concepts had been quite profitable, previously trading as wet-led businesses... Anyway, the carvery operation did ok but the grill concept was struggling... What Bruce did was survive through divide and rule... He tore through a succession of managers in both brands, blaming their under-performance upon every successive incumbent... He actually set the carvery brand up against the grill brand... there was no knowledge sharing or swapping of people... just pure loathing actually... all nicely stoked up by Bruce... I'm sure he was saying to the board 'don't worry, I'll sort this rabble out' – and they believed him... Bruce had worked his way up the operation and – because of his food experience – was regarded as a safe pair of hands... Nobody on the Board had been anywhere remotely near a kitchen in their lives... In the end though, he ran out of excuses. What we did was sort out the carvery brand and disband the grill operation, eventually buying a nicely positioned grill concept that has subsequently gone on to become one of the market leaders! ... Worryingly, I know that Bruce popped up somewhere else later but nobody I rated would ever go and work for him...'

5.2 Resource Starvation

Incompetent leadership can have a devastating effect on hitherto successful brands but their demise is hastened if they are starved of the oxygen - in the form of 'hard' financial and 'soft' human resources - needed to progress. Often organisations are subject to resource starvation because of a perverse domino effect. A blip in trading or a downward trend in sales causes brand leaders to cut back on property investment and reduce labour costs in order to recover the bottom line. In the short term, the profit lines (operational, EBITDA and PBT) look better; but over the long term, customers notice a marked deterioration in environment and service. Sales decelerate, going from bad to worse, but the brand leadership - lacking a plan B - continues to strip costs out of the business. The upshot of such draconian action is that the brand begins to look and act shabbily, losing the confidence of both its employees and customers.

Causal Factors

As stated, a protracted lack of financial and human resources undermines the functional and emotional benefits of the brand for both employees and customers. The brand cannot retain its distinctiveness in relation to its competitive set; rather, its differentiation now stems from being so awful! But apart from incompetent brand leadership (see above), what are the main causal factors behind resource starvation?

- ◘ **Economic adjustments** - the first thing that triggers resource anaemia within organisations is macroeconomic movements. Events such as the Great Recession in the developed world of 2008-14 had a profound effect on consumer buying behaviour in food service, with consumers migrating to value-led offers due to squeezes in discretionary income. More recently - as confidence has returned - there has been a trend towards trading up within the market. Food service offers have been caught out by both economic adjustments: value offers faring well during straightened times (for 'small treat occasions') and 'better' offers prospering in more affluent circumstances (for 'social' and 'celebratory' occasions). Macro-movements in consumer behaviour, caused by seismic economic events, can cause companies to take short-term cost-cutting measures to 'get to the other side'; but this process may alienate loyal customers, some of whom are then lost to the brand permanently.
- ◘ **Lines of credit** - given the high failure rate of hospitality businesses, banks are loath to lend money to 'entrepreneurs' who believe that they

have the next big food service idea. This is understandable and, indeed, one of the principal reasons why crowdfunding has been such a popular way for food service entrepreneurs to raise initial seed capital in recent times. The issue for successful brands is different. Having established a strong consumer franchise, they might have hit a few roadblocks through inappropriate site selection and/or experienced temporary cash-flow problems caused by rapid expansion. It is at this point that the brand owner might expect some support from their bank in the form of extended credit terms or a larger overdraft, given that they have already demonstrated some record of success. The reality is, however – and this was certainly the case during the Great Recession – that banks will seldom stand completely behind the brand unless further collateral or personal guarantees are given. Sadly, the fledgling existence of many promising brands has been terminated by unsympathetic bankers.

- **Competitive pressure** – the third thing that has a direct impact on resource allocation within food service brands is high levels of competitive pressure in local micro-markets that 'strip sales'. Instead of reacting to this pressure through investing in changes to the brand's marketing mix – providing a strong competitive response that improves the chances of longevity – policy makers can press the panic button by putting prices up or taking costs out of the business; a response that (if sustained) will lead to perceptions of brand dilution in the eyes of the customer. Again, this course of action threatens terminal decline.

- **Ownership gorging** – another factor that can cause starvation is moves by the owner to strip the business for the purposes of short-termist profit gorging. Why? The brand owner might need the funds to prop up failing businesses elsewhere or achieve short-term hikes in profitability to increase the EBITDA multiple of the business for sale and/or market listing purposes. Prospective buyers (of the enterprise or stock) should examine the 'gearing run-rate' of the business before they transact with the owner or they will receive a nasty shock when they find that they have bought a hollowed out entity that requires a high degree of capital and revenue investment to survive. Caveat emptor!

- **Costs of doing business** – the final factor that can affect hard and soft resource distribution within the brand is rising input costs that – on the basis of the brand's positioning – threaten its long-term viability. Costs such as rental increases, local tax hikes (i.e. rates in the UK), minimum wage, energy and ingredient inflation can dramatically change the sustainability of the brand's business model if it is unable to offset them with average spend per head and productivity increases that do not affect customer perceptions of quality and service. Indeed, one of the features of a truly great brand is its ability to absorb increased costs whilst simultaneously increasing sales, margins and levels of customer satisfaction! Those that can't are in peril.

Remedies

The fact is, resources are scarce and need to be sparingly applied in most businesses. However, in some businesses they are more plentiful than in others: in instances where they are becoming increasingly scarce, what is to be done?

- **Target scarce resources** – the first thing that can be done in organisations with rapidly diminishing financial resources is to target what remains at key locations to test whether or not the brand can be turned around by taking a slightly different tack. Having proof-tested this approach – and hopefully found it to be highly accretive – brand leadership can put the case for further investment or more funds (see the TGI Friday's case study in Chapter 6, below).
- **Hoard resources** – another solution is to build up a war chest for when times turn sour. Admittedly, this needs a high degree of foresight and planning. It can involve either the hoarding of cash (difficult in private-equity contexts) and/or investing heavily in assets during the good times to build a quality estate that can weather under-investment during the bad times.
- **Ride out the dip** – another option open to brand leaders is to keep the faith – riding out the dip in performance (caused by extraneous economic circumstances) by continuing to invest in the brand – accepting lower margins and profit as a consequence – in order to emerge stronger on the other side. Admittedly, this easier done in more private, rather than public, ownership circumstances. In the public arena, a requirement for quarterly performance updates almost forces brand leaders to take draconian short-term action to show growth; private-ownership contexts allow a more long-term perspective to be applied.
- **White knight saviour** – in situations where the brand is being skimmed by unscrupulous owners and denied funds by unsympathetic lenders, 'white knight' saviours who recognise the real value that can be released through buying and then investing in the brand can remedy seemingly irredeemable situations.

CASE STUDY 16 – **STARVING BRANDS IN THE US**
Frank Steed

Frank Steed has had a long and illustrious career in the US food service industry, building and leading some of the sector's most successful brands over the past thirty years. He now runs his own consultancy advising owners and leaders on brand development (particularly within the franchising domain).

At present in the US, there is a trend – rather like the manufacturing industry beforehand – for activist investors and VCs to sink their (or more likely their investors') money into highly cash-generative food service concepts... Often their stewardship, with its short-termist value engineering perspective, ends in disaster for the assets... either during their tenure or later on down the track when the brand has passed a point of no return... But why does their ownership commonly end in terminal decline and failure?

1. **'Economic' strategie**s – the first thing to say is that activist investors and VCs are often driven by an instant-profit motive... For instance, at present one of the world's greatest franchised food service brands has agitating investors that want it to 'unlock value' through selling its extensive freehold estate... This is in spite of the fact that the franchisor – who acts as a landlord to all of its franchisees – has exemplary control of its franchise system through this arrangement, making it easy for them to enact changes quickly and turf out freeriders and shirkers within the system with relative ease... Selling these assets off might generate huge cash windfalls (in terms of stock buy backs) for the activists, but the loss of direct control (not to mention the expense of a rented estate) would irrevocably change this brand's business model... Also, during my long career in the industry I have often come across instances where new VC owners have overlaid stretch-based financial models upon perfectly sound operational models: cutting labour, conducting sale and leasebacks, procuring tertiary instead of prime sites, reducing entry costs for franchisees through dumbing down the brand etc. All actions that eventually lead to one conclusion – slow, tortuous decline followed by death! ...
2. **Goal misalignment** – the question arises as to why some VCs pursue such strategies... after all, they are populated by perfectly sane and rational people... The reason is that their time horizons on paybacks

and returns are extremely short... They inevitably have to beat the returns of other forms of investment instrument: to justify their fees and keep investor funds flowing, they need to demonstrate stellar compound growth... Inevitably, however, their goals are completely at odds with management and (in franchised contexts) franchisees... In franchised environments where franchisees have typically signed up for 20-year agreements, the goals of VCs – short-term financial gorging – is completely at odds with a franchisee's need for a long-term sustainable fully invested/supported business model... Sometimes – because of this misalignment – the relationship between VC owner and its franchise system becomes extremely fractious and toxic, a state of disharmony that can only do major long-term damage to the consistency, reputation and quality of the brand...

3. **Management credibility** – in franchised systems, the brand's management is often a piggy in the middle between the VC owner and franchisees... it is really hard for them not to be seen either as hired guns or totally impotent by franchisees... I have seen CEOs operating in these circumstances who have been ridiculed and ignored by long-timer franchisees who perceive them as only passing through... This lack of credibility makes the job of managing standards and developing the brand extremely difficult... another factor that eventually contributes to the decline/demise of a promising brand...

5.3 Concept Obsolescence

The final reason we attribute to brand failure is obsolescence: the concept no longer possesses any viable consumer franchise. Returning to our definition of successful brands, we can reverse it to define brands that perish: *dying food service brands fail to have a compelling culinary positioning, and provide indistinct emotional and functional benefits that fail to meet changing customer needs, feelings and aspirations, thus resulting in rejection, switching and detraction!* Such brands have reached a point of no return because they are perceived as outdated and have been overtaken and usurped by fresher, younger upstarts. They have no voice or traction within the marketplace. A loyal hard-core rump user group might have stayed on, providing brand leaders with some (illusory!) cause for optimism that the brand has a future. However in truth, these users only remain because they feel disenfranchised and detached from the rest of the market and because (curiously) they have a Moonie-style loyalty that inures them from the negative aspects of the brand.

Common Reasons

But what are the most common explanations for brand obsolescence? Accepting the fact that this chapter's previous sections (on incompetent leadership and resource starvation) highlighted factors that contribute to driving brands into this parlous state, what are the *customer-driven* reasons for their disappearance from the food service landscape? In the Introduction, we outlined some consumer mega-trends, suggesting that customers are becoming more **informed** (able to access comparative information), **itinerant** (more willing to switch, given knowledge of the available options) and **impatient** (more inclined to immediate rather deferred gratification).

- **Outmoded cuisine** – at the heart of the demise of any food service concept lies a failure to wow customers with food quality levels (this being the foremost customer requirement in food service). Customer perceptions of food quality don't necessarily only relate to views concerning the standard of the food (i.e. hot, cooked to specification etc.); they also encapsulate feelings regarding taste and contemporaneousness (for instance, whether the food is bland and boring in comparison to that of other brands). Brands that are failing generally have cuisine that is not only badly executed, but is perceived as being inferior and totally off trend compared to that of other food service offers.

- **Outdated service-delivery system** – another factor that customers pinpoint (highlighted in the mega-trends above) as a major attractor/ detractor in food service brands is speed of service. Long queues and high wait times in service (i.e. slow seating processes, ponderous order taking, tardy food and beverage delivery and cheque settlement) are major detractors which can really erode the reputation of the brand; particularly when competitors have demonstrably sharper order fulfilment processes in place. The term 'full table service' is perceived as an oxymoron in some concepts: service is perceived by customers as being poorer when they are allegedly waited upon 'hand and foot' compared to contexts where they are expected to complete elements of the service cycle themselves; in self-serve buffet and/ or fast casual contexts, for instance. Increasing perceptions of accessibility through decreasing barriers to entry has been a major achievement of the fast casual dining movement. Brands that have remained stuck in the past by failing to reduce the number of service steps or speeding up the cycle through technology (e.g. handheld ordering systems) have placed their business model at serious risk.

- ☐ **Low perceived value** – we have previously highlighted the need for food service concepts to keep the major elements of their value proposition in balance. That is to say product quality, environment, service and price must be viewed holistically rather than as a sum of distinct parts. Deadly combinations will destroy the food service brand if, for instance, there is an obvious incongruence between these factors (i.e. if what customers are being asked to pay is out of kilter with product quality, amenity and service). The problem that failing food service brands have on this count is of finding how to shift perceptions concerning the value proposition when they can ill afford to rectify the imbalance (because it would 'blow up' the P&L). Obviously, food service brands should always seek to give benefits that provide a high perceived value to the customers at minimal cost to themselves. But in some failing brands, inexpensive gestures are futile and will do little to resolve terminal perceptions of low perceived value.

- ☐ **Unloved** – the final factor that drives a brand towards extinction is simple: customers have fallen out of love with it. Not only does it now fail to meet any of their basic needs, it no longer elicits strong feelings of attachment or aspiration. Customers feel ambivalent about the brand – it has slipped way down their repertoire of choices because they really don't care for what it offers and stands for. It means nothing to them. Worse than that, brand employees share and reinforce their feelings. Front-line service providers, who are supposed to personify the brand and bring it alive, now act in a detached, disillusioned and dispassionate manner because they lack any deep emotional connection with a brand, which they sense is sleepwalking into oblivion. They display few signs of excitement and joy 'on the floor' and this is either consciously or subconsciously picked up by customers, degrading their experience, leading to their fatal decision (for the brand) not to return.

Choices

What are the remedies for brands sliding into obsolescence? The next chapter will delve into how brand leaders can revive a brand through re-engaging employees, sharpening execution and refreshing the proposition. But in the case of brands that have advanced beyond the pale, what choices are available to their leaders at this juncture?

- **Re-brand** – brand leaders can opt for a total re-brand, remaining within the category with a re-crafted proposition. They design a new compelling culinary concept that addresses the same consumer channel, trial it in existing sites and – if it works – back it into the entire estate. Can such a course of action work? Replacing the existing estate with a new start-up concept is a highly complex process requiring multiple resources. It is possible, if the brand owner has deep pockets – but the chances of success are extremely low!

- **Substitution** – one option that that is frequently deployed by multiple brand owners is the substitution of a failing brand with concepts from their wider brand portfolio. Given the fact that they are likely to have liabilities and covenant responsibilities in a number of 'failing brand' sites, they are able to minimise losses through a process of replacement: swapping out the failed brand for new vibrant concepts that add immediate value to the overall portfolio. They must take care, however, that they do not make matters worse by putting the wrong branded 'solution' out of their portfolio into the wrong site. Often, multi-brand owners will attack portfolio underperformance with the wrong brands, making highly expensive mistakes that exacerbate rather than resolve the problem (often because some sites may just not be suitable for *any* food service offer).

- **Honourable administration** – finally, the brand leader can accept the inevitable (although they rarely do!). Either the brand wasn't a brand in the first place – merely a whimsical here-today, gone-tomorrow fad that never stood any chance of longevity – or the erstwhile successful concept has run its course. The brand leader should dissolve the assets in an orderly fashion (see above), minimising the pain and fall out for all stakeholders.

CASE STUDY 17 – **BERNI INNS: HOW AN ICONIC BRAND BECAME OBSOLESCENT**
Alan Jackson and Tony Hughes

Alan Jackson is the founder of Beefeater and was MD during its halcyon years. He is a renowned senior industry figure in UK hospitality, having started up and led some of the UK's most successful food service brands and concepts over the past forty years. Here, he reflects on the key reasons for the end of Berni.

Berni – Its End!

Berni was not unique in its reasons for failure... Many of today's most prestigious companies have failed to recognise and react to consumer changes in the same way that Berni failed to do years ago.

Berni was a product of the recovery of the UK in the 1960s when eating out was starting to establish itself for the mass market. It offered a known product at a known price and – most important to a country still steeped in the class structure – it introduced a casual, relaxed dining atmosphere for 'ordinary people' – all on the base attributes of a multi-site branded product with – importantly – *no surprises... real value for money!* ... However, the original footprint concept of two restaurants, two bars and two menus *had significant failings*... First, it was inefficient in terms of overhead cost control and efficiency... Second, it was 'divisive' for the diner, who often had to compromise on which restaurant they used because of the slightly differing menus...

Beefeater (which I started in 1973/4 in Whitbread) recognised that a change was necessary and that Berni had failed to see how consumer taste and demographics were evolving... I guess you ignore or fail to understand/accept the customer's view at your peril! ... We therefore evolved the structure: ONE RESTAURANT, ONE BAR, ONE MENU... This produced a significant R.O.I. for Whitbread... It also reflected the evolution of consumer taste... we valued family trade: children became an important part of our offering, unlike Berni's rigid approach which failed to recognise the value and growth of the market for children eating out alongside their parents.

The original Beefeater USP was our semi-theatrical design that used the cube of the building, had relaxed informal service and a great product range... We were smaller at the time and tried harder, recognising how fast the eating-out public was evolving... and we watched the competition! ... Also our staff were highly motivated: our waiting staff were *usually* English, *usually* friendly but were, *above all* interested in what the customer wanted – they had the keys to the kingdom... Our success with Beefeater laid not only the foundations for the acquisition of Berni but also the genesis of the provision of budget accommodation on Beefeater sites through access to a brand the public could trust...

So ultimately, the purchase of Berni was a reflection of its management's lack of focus and recognition that change and evolution were essential to grow market share... All of which sounds perhaps familiar to a number of our major high-street retailers today!

As Operations Director of Whitbread, Tony Hughes (co-author of this book) converted a huge number of Berni Inns into Beefeater Restaurants in the mid-1980s. Here, he reflects upon the demise of the iconic 'first-mover' steakhouse chain in the UK.

Background history – established in 1955, Berni Inn was a chain of iconic British steakhouses. It was founded by the Berni brothers (Frank and Aldo) who – opening the first Berni Inn at the Rummer pub in the centre of Bristol – based the chain upon restaurants they had visited in the US. Essentially, Berni Inns introduced the post-war British public to its own domestic restaurant chain, which came with its own stylised design – its iconic Tudor-looking false oak beams and white walls. It developed a loyal and regular following and quickly expanded, first throughout Bristol, then through much of the rest of the UK. The chain offered slick service and value for money, achieved partly by offering only a limited meat-based menu and a relatively small wine list. A typical menu comprised of: starters (melon boat with maraschino cherry, or prawn cocktail – pate was added later), main course (steak, gammon steak or plaice with chips and peas) and dessert (Black Forest gateau or a choice of cheeses: danish blue, stilton or cheddar) plus Irish coffee and After Eight mints. Unlike other restaurants at the time, Berni Inns did not do their own butchery but bought in quality steak from Argentina. Behind the scenes, staff training manuals ensured consistency of standards and quality; stock control systems merely concentrated on counting high-value items (prawns, steaks and wine). To prevent 'cheque shock', food bills were separated from cash drinks sales, meaning customers had a real perception of value! By 1970, the chain comprised 147 hotels and restaurants and was the largest food chain outside the USA. The chain was sold to Grand Metropolitan for £14.5m in 1970 and then sold to us at Whitbread in 1985, after which we converted the outlets into our own Beefeater and Brewers Fayre restaurants. So why did this iconic brand disappear from the UK foodscape?

Reasons for demise – in my mind, there were four reasons why Berni eventually disappeared as a brand, despite having previously held a position of *absolute* category leadership:

1. **Unloved** – when Berni was taken over by Grand Met in 1970, it joined a conglomerate containing a hotchpotch of other businesses. Frankly, the new owners did not care enough about nurturing and developing the brand. The menu became muddled – 'food from around the world' – and the service cycle (where covers were turned by 'offering coffee in the lounge') came to be seen as outdated. Staff became disillusioned and left [see below]... In addition, customers fell out of love with the brand! When we bought the brand in 1985 I did a couple of new 'Classic Berni' trial sites – taking it back to basics – with *brilliant* steaks. What I found was that, although customers had a degree of nostalgia for the brand, the world had moved on. Younger generations didn't want to eat where their parents had eaten.

2. **Fast followers** – Berni was founded with passion by two brothers but copied with zeal by the nationals, Whitbread (Beefeater Restaurants) and Allied (Cavalier Steakhouses). They copied both the hardware (interior design, menus, service cycle) and recruited the software (key Berni personnel that had huge tacit operational knowledge). These competitors were far more focused than Grand Met in evolving and developing a steakhouse offer that – having taken the best from Berni – really matched changing consumer needs.

3. **Distribution access** – at one point during my time as a Beefeater Operations Director, we were opening at a rate of two new sites a week – Berni did not have this luxury! We had nearly 6,000 freehold sites within the Whitbread estate to choose from, so we were able to overtake Berni in terms of scale pretty rapidly. The freehold element was particularly important: it meant that we could command higher per-site returns than Berni (many of their sites being leasehold or tenanted).

4. **Competitor aggression** – being successful for so long had led to an air of complacency within Berni. For an aggressive newcomer, it's easier to play catch up and, as the number two in the market, to focus upon outdoing the competition. At Beefeater we were motivated and aggressive both in terms of roll-out and pricing (entering and winning many discount wars to attract customers from Berni). We made it our sole mission to out-perform, out-trade and win customers from Berni... Eventually, when they 'blinked', we bought them and substituted their sites with our brands.

Final Thoughts

The core theme of this chapter has been how and why food service brands perish. It has argued that there are – in our view – three major reasons why food service brands fail the test of time: incompetent leadership, resource starvation and product obsolescence. Often these three factors are inextricably bound together - incompetent leaders misallocating or plundering scarce resources, leading to brand extinction. However, there is one factor that resonates throughout these sections that, above all else, causes brands to fail: **loss of reputation**. Great food service brands are (as previous chapters have demonstrated) scrupulously crafted by Originators, rolled-out and systemised by Escalators and incrementally improved by Evolvers. Also, it could be argued that it is the Originator who creates a brand reputation, whilst the Escalator builds it and the Evolver sustains/augments it. Essentially, brands which perish have lost their reputation: both employees and customers have lost trust and faith in them. Such a brand no longer delivers against its brand promise because it has lost (or mislaid) its core purpose by becoming diverted or distracted. In summary, in our view, the most important asset a food service brand has is its reputation; once this is lost it is almost impossible to regain!

Once singular brands have totally lost their reputation and are beyond redemption, the final stage of their lifecycle is either ignominious bankruptcy or managed closure. In the former case, there have been plenty of cases of food service brands in the UK going into sudden administration, calling in receivers to retrieve some value from the distressed assets. In this 'perish' scenario, brand leaders left holding the baby are often branded pariahs because they are perceived (rightly or wrongly) to have been the principal architects of the brand's demise. Sometimes these executives have difficulty - especially if they've misled stakeholders - finding employment at a similar level again because they are perceived as damaged goods. With regards to the latter case - those brand leaders that manage an orderly exit - extraordinary skill is required in managing the wind down the enterprise. Here, brand leaders must manage the anxiety and fear of a number of stakeholders by communicating sensitively and honestly - not least to brand staff whose first thought is 'what happens to me!?' As improbable as it might seem, some brand leaders come out of the dissolution phase of a brand's demise with their own reputation intact because they have tried to be transparent and even-handed with all stakeholders who - in actual fact - had probably known for some time that the writing was on the wall.

But is perish the inevitable conclusion to the brand lifecycle or can this nose dive towards disappearance be prevented in the first place? The next chapter, 'Revive', will look at how brands can and do pull themselves back from the brink.

CHAPTER 6 **Revive**

SIX

Food service brands that have enjoyed a strong consumer franchise needn't perish. They can avoid termination by being revived through transformational change – a process that is made easier if the organisation itself recognises the need for dramatic reconstructive surgery. The likelihood is, however, that the brand will be in a state of paralysis and/or denial. Why? Brand members have either given up hope that there is any chance of reversal in the brand's downward trajectory; or during the slow descent into oblivion, they have ignored the signs of deterioration and disintegration. They have made ample excuses for underperformance, continuing to apply tried and tested methods that worked in the past in the vain hope that the environment around them will change back to the way it was in the past. Some units within the food service brand might still be performing well, providing brand members in these areas with little incentive to change, whilst the true state of the brand's sickness might have been deliberately been hidden from the rest of the portfolio by naive brand leaders who have blind faith in the fact that things will right themselves.

It is into this arena that the transformational leader strides with the express objective of reviving the brand. This individual – whom we term the 'Reviver' – is usually an outsider. Lacking any sentimental attachment to the past, internal political loyalties or commitment to particular courses of action, Revivers can dispassionately assess what needs to be done and despatch their mission with 'violent intent'. They confront a perilous and complex situation where the brand needs revitalising from a declining base: a process which requires simultaneous rationalisation and building activities! To this extent, the Reviver requires a subtle bled of both leadership and management skills and capabilities. S/he must be capable of installing a new vision and sense of hope whilst implementing new systems, routines and measures. To this extent, the Reviver needs to be both participative and hands on in their approach, creating ownership and accountability through involving and delegating whilst scrupulously attending to the detail of the transformational plan and its execution.

Accepting this, what do we regard as being the essential activities that effective Revivers should attend to do during this turnaround stage?

We believe that great Revivers of food service brands do three things particularly well. First, they *galvanise the organisation* with a sense of purpose and mission with regards to the transformational change process. Second, they *sharpen execution* within the brand through renewed focus, measurement and vigour. Third, they *refresh the proposition* of the brand, creating a sense of vision that is consistent with the past but, at the same time, relevant to the challenges/opportunities of the present and future. These will now be considered in turn after the case study below, which is an outstanding example of how to turn around a failing brand.

CASE STUDY 18 – **TGI FRIDAY'S: REVIVING A BRAND**
Karen Forester

Karen Forester has been the CEO of TGI Friday's, UK since 2007 when she was parachuted in by new owners to turn it around. During her time in charge, she is widely acknowledged by industry experts as having orchestrated one of the great brand revivals within the history of UK hospitality. Karen has had a long and successful career in the industry, including senior executive positions in a number of the UK's top pub restaurant brands.

When I was appointed as leader of TGI Friday's in 2007 it was in a sorry state in terms of people, product, infrastructure and positioning. Its previous owner had fallen out of love with the brand... Within its multi-brand portfolio, TGI Friday's was very much the poor relation, generally perceived as a management stepping stone for bigger brand appointments... Two metrics stood out at the time – symbolising the desperate state the brand had reached: team turnover had reached 157% and less than one in three team members were fully trained and certified to their jobs! ... Frankly, the previous management had been 'hiring hands not personalities and hearts and minds' trained and equipped to deliver **memorable guest experiences**... Investment in the brand had been halted, there was no roll-out plan and, financially, sales and profit were in decline... Today, team turnover hovers around 40%; team engagement is at an all-time high (we won the *Sunday Times'* 'Top Big Company to Work For' Award in 2014); all of our restaurants achieved a 5-star 'Score on the Doors' environmental health rating in

2015 (an industry first within the casual dining sector!); and we have opened 25 new restaurants and increased the EDITDA of the company from £4.2m to £30m (2015 calendar year) during the course of the turnaround. Looking back, I would highlight the following building blocks as being instrumental to the brand's revival:

1. **Restoring pride amongst our people** – TGI Friday's had been famous for giving great emotional experiences to its guests... it was renowned for its 'big personality': the fun, release and exuberance of its team; the boldness and generosity of its food; the flair and excitement of its bars. But the starting point was always the team – they were the brand experience – they were the defining personality of the brand... We could fix the product and the environment; it was the team we had to start with first... How did we do this? ... When I arrived, I could see that the team felt unloved: for instance, the previous owner had dumbed down the uniform, taking away the iconic 'stripes' that recognised outstanding service performance... our teamers kept saying to me 'bring back the stripes!'... Symbolically, I re-instituted them in 2009 through a programme called 'Earn Your Stripes' where teamers had to achieve certification... then were recognised at graduation awards ceremonies... For me, this marked the symbolic rebirth of the company and was the start of the turnaround... It restored a sense of team aspiration and buzz which translated into providing far better emotional service and higher sales/profits... The hockey stick of our revival definitely started here...

2. **Improving standards and execution** – in parallel with this, we had to raise our standards: frankly, our restaurants were dirty... How did we do this? ... First, we scrubbed everything until it shone and mended things that were broken! .... Second, we introduced operational 'deep dive' inspections where we thoroughly scrutinise cleanliness and test the knowledge/skills of all our team to ensure units are 'ready'... Third, in November – prior to the key Xmas trading period – when these deep dives have ensured we are set up in terms of quality, the executive team goes out on site visits at peak sessions to 'catch and reward people doing great things!'... Fourth, we retrain and recertify all our team every year to make sure that they have the right 'fit' (i.e. will and skill) to do their jobs...

3. **Clear vision and values** – in order to underpin our transformation, we needed to drive consistent behaviours towards achieving a common purpose... we needed to get away from the corporate jargon of the previous owners... The vision we finally settled upon

was *'our people are family, our guests become friends, our competitors envy us'*... Again, our team was the start point of this vision. We wanted to instil a sense of belonging, engagement and attachment which would translate into 'wowing' our guests (ultimately resulting in higher sales/profits)... Our values (which were endorsed/recognised by certain 'pin' categories that could be worn with pride by team members) became *Pride* (a contagious belief in our brand), *Passion* (pursuing excellence on our stage), *Personality* (seeking opportunities to shine) and *Protection* (safety first)... The top team that I brought on board for the turnaround (a blend of internal and external talent) were all hires that exemplified and bought into these values – individuals who had professional entrepreneurial rather than corporate mindsets...

4. **Refreshed and restored proposition** – what generally happens with failing brands is that they merge and become relatively indistinct from their competitive set... This is particularly the case if a brand is part of a multi-brand portfolio... Under its old ownership, food ingredients had been cost engineered through central purchasing decisions: for instance, TGI Friday's iconic Jack Daniel's glaze – previously imported from the US – was replaced with an inferior UK substitute... Also, its iconic fries were sourced domestically for cost reasons... We reversed these decisions: Jack Daniel's glaze and our fries are now imported (once again) from the US... Moreover, the menu was suffering from 'spread' as we attempted to follow our competitors: when I arrived, we had a national marketing campaign publicising our new 'East meets West' fusion offer. I stopped this immediately... Cost engineering also meant that plastic had replaced leather covering on our seats – again, something that we reversed... We had to restore the brand to its former glory. Bad decisions, made on the basis of panic and confusion, had allowed it to drift away from its sweet spot... I was determined to re-differentiate the brand, giving our guests an experience that could not be replicated elsewhere!

5. **Roll-out confidence** – during the beginning of our revival we had an opportunity to open a new site in the Trafford Centre... I convinced the board it was the right thing to do... Since opening six years ago, it has performed consistently within our top three sites and is the top-ranked restaurant (in terms of turnover) at this location... Clearly, this was a massive risk that paid off (literally paying for itself within 14 months!)... What it gave us was, first, a new template to roll out and, second, renewed confidence that we could expand the brand...

It is my view that we are now in a white space that we can command... we are clear category leaders within a category of one... we are **THE** *experiential brand*! ... The dangers we face are that – as we grow in size and scale – we become too bureaucratic and the dynamism and thrill of the turnaround years might dissipate... I see it as my job to keep stepping in and making sure decisions are taken quickly and meetings are kept to a minimum... To keep energy levels up, reiterating the fact that we have huge growth potential still within us! ... In the future, technology will be a great enabler for our like-for-like sales growth... but the one thing that we must never lose sight of again is that Friday's provides a high-end emotional experience... We don't really need to advertise... our guests are our raving advocates, departing with fantastic memories... It is the people factor in this brand that counts most... hiring, developing, motivating and retaining great service personalities lies at the heart of this brand... something that most of our competitors will always struggle to replicate! ...

6.1 Galvanise Organisation

Our starting point for the transformation process lies within the organisation itself. Enterprises that are experiencing seemingly terminal decline are populated with people who have lost confidence and belief. As food service businesses are performance orientated, this pessimism has catastrophic consequences if it infects the perceptions of key stakeholders and commentators (customers, suppliers, shareholders, industry press and so forth). The Revivers must therefore focus their primary efforts upon galvanising the organisation so that it regains its mojo! How do they do this? Academics have drawn a clear distinction between incremental and transformational renewal: the former being characterised as a patient form of continuous improvement (see Chapter 4, 'Evolve') and the latter as dramatic 'shock therapy'. Nevertheless, like continuous improvement, business transformation can be conceived as a planned process.

In our view, the one thing that separates leaders from managers is that managers are 'all about executing the today' whilst leaders 'are all about facilitating change for the tomorrow'. With regards to change, the most cited scholar in this area – John Kotter (1996) – advocates that leaders should transition their organisation through eight key phases (grouped into three key stages: 'creating the climate', 'engaging and enabling' and 'implementing and sustaining') in order to effect impactful and long-lasting change. We believe his model and its key insights are important enough to recite here, given their relevance to food service concept revival:

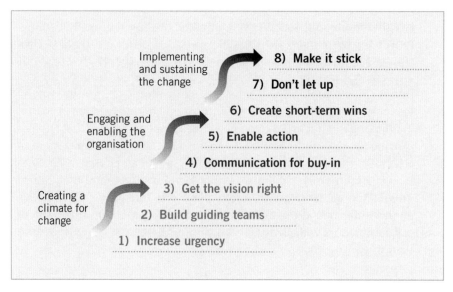

Figure 6 **Eight Phases of Change Model**

- ◘ **Increase urgency** – in order to overcome complacency, misplaced feelings of security must be eliminated through the creation of a 'burning platform' (i.e. technological disruption or 'barbarians at the gates').
- ◘ **Build a guiding team** – a team with a shared purpose and understanding of the scale of the task accompanied with a belief in a successful outcome should be brought together. This strong coalition should be furnished with the necessary skills, reputation and network to lead the change agenda.
- ◘ **Get the vision right** – the team must build a vision that bridges the current and future state. The vision ('where we want to get to') must be meaningful and compelling, underpinned by sound strategy and tactics.
- ◘ **Communication for buy-in** – consistent and coherent messaging concerning the change, which addresses the 'what's in it for me?' question for employees, must be effectively disseminated across the whole organisation.
- ◘ **Enable action** – empower change agents by removing obstacles whilst simultaneously adjusting systems and/or structures that work against the vision.

- **Create short-term wins** – because the change process might be lengthy and painful, recipients should be encouraged to feel that the plan has positive momentum and the final destination will be worthwhile by the visibility of a number of short-term wins.
- **Don't let up** – gains should be consolidated but a relentless pace should continue in order to generate further gains.
- **Make it stick** – once major changes have been made, they must be made permanent by being embedded within the corporate culture ('the way in which we do things around here').

Essentially, Kotter and other academics working in the transformational change field are pretty united in the view that organisations should concentrate upon what they can do rather than obsessively focusing upon the competition – or blaming it for their predicament. But what do we believe to be the base qualifiers and differentiators that galvanise an organisation during the revival process, leading to the success of the transformation plan?

Galvanising Qualifiers

Whilst we would echo many of the points made in Kotter's model above, it is our belief that the key qualifying factors in sparking a revival are as follows:

- **Paint a picture** – the first thing that the Reviver should do is awaken the organisation to the enormous market opportunity that still remains, whilst emphasising the pain that people will have to go through in order to crystallise it. To this extent, the Reviver's role is remarkably similar to that of the Originator (see Chapter 2) in the creation phase of the brand. The Reviver must cast a narrative spell over his/her followers with a compelling vision for the future of the brand. This is more effectively achieved through stories that paint a picture of the 'promised land' destination – making the discomfort of journey seem somehow palatable – rather than dry, rational explanations and numbers.
- **Big objectives** – nevertheless, given that the Reviver is attempting to transform the organisation, s/he must effect a paradigm shift in attitudes and behaviours by putting in place bold goals and objectives. Why? They return the enterprise back to its pioneering start-up and roll-out phase when brand members were encouraged to believe that anything was possible. By putting aspirational objectives in place, the

Reviver is signalling that s/he is intent on step-changing the organisation and that anybody who 'stays on board the bus' is going to have to dramatically up their game. Naturally, whilst stretching, these objectives should be within the realms of possibility, backed up with a credible plan as to how they might be achieved.

- ◘ **Potent symbolism** – in order to get a fast start, the Reviver can take a number of quick actions that will symbolise the fact that things are going to be different around here. If s/he has inherited a bureaucratic, ossified organisation, s/he can immediately set the new tone by despatching decisions swiftly and holding brief, purposeful meetings in which people are held *individually* to account for what has been agreed collectively. Instant reductions in, and removal of, hierarchy, deference and status will also have a profound effect on brand-member perceptions regarding fairness, equity and openness. Revivers never underestimate the potency of making quick, symbolic changes that, first, signal the way in which they want business to be professionally transacted during their tenure; and second, set the behavioural foundations for major transformational change further down the line.

- ◘ **Multi-disciplinary team** – Kotter's framework, above, envisages a 'guiding coalition' coming together to act as a major catalyst for change. We go beyond this, by suggesting that Revivers – if they are to stand any chance of success during their transformational mission – require a team of 'all the talents' in order to reignite the brand. Why? What needs to be done, both in terms of sharpening execution and refreshing the proposition (see the sections below), requires a multitude of key skills and capabilities. It is advisable, however, that the Reviver does not solely draw upon other outsiders to populate his/her new multi-disciplinary team. A blend of insiders (who tacitly understand the brand's archaeology and culture) and outsiders (who possess professional expertise that fills gaps in the organisation's capability) should be melded together by the Reviver to achieve a 'best of each' scenario. For sure, if the Reviver relies only upon his/her team of turnaround outsiders, s/he will most likely alienate the rest of the organisation, setting up a 'them and us' situation which will impede efforts for a (relatively) quick transformation.

Galvanising Differentiators

It is often assumed by many managers that the hardest part of any business transformation is the restructuring process, which involves reallocating and rationalising tasks and roles. However, these visible changes are far easier to implement than the main determinants of transformational success: behaviours and culture. These are highly intangible and invisible forces which the Reviver must address, transitioning brand members swiftly through the change curve so that they think and act in a manner consistent with the realities of the new organisational paradigm. The factors above will assist in shifting behaviours; but what are the differentiators for Revivers attempting to galvanise the organisation into rapid action?

◻ **Personal sacrifice** – the main thing that characterises successful Revivers is their ability to demonstrate and endure authentic personal sacrifice during the transformation process, signalling a 'we're all in it together' mentality. Working long hours, expending tremendous amounts of energy and taking little in return (i.e. spurning or re-distributing large short-term personal bonuses and incentives), the Reviver inspires genuine followership during the tough tasks and choices that lie ahead. S/he does not make sacrifices that are token gestures and exposed as opportunistic PR exercises further on down the line (in Annual Report disclosures, for instance) but real sacrifices that are respected and imitated by brand members during what can be a tough and brutal process of revival. Through their own signalling behaviour, Revivers are able to send out a strong message regarding the desirability of being hard on costs – that saving money is a noble cause and 'everyday low cost' should always precede 'everyday low price'.

◻ **Eliminate saboteurs** – the second most important thing that marks out effective Revivers is their ability to smoke out and despatch saboteurs intent on derailing the transformation process. Generally, there are four types of resistors during change programmes: protestors (who openly declare their opposition to change), zombies (who have no opinions of their own and are easily led by opponents of change), survivors (who maintain a self-interested strategy of malevolent silence) and saboteurs (who covertly conspire and undermine). Within these categories, the saboteurs are the most dangerous because they wilfully (and secretly) scheme to block and derail any changes that threaten their own position or the status quo. In order to flush out this enemy, in addition to monitoring behaviours, the Reviver must examine hard outcomes. Where is the change being blocked, halted or diluted? By whom and when? S/he must then act decisively to move malevolent saboteurs from the field of play.

- **Over-index recognition** – another feature of effective Revivers is their public recognition of great follower behaviours and practices during the transformation process. Earlier on in the book we referred to the need for brand leaders to recognise outstanding effort though tangible rewards, which recipients can show to their peers, friends and families, thereby increasing their levels of pride and self-esteem. Revivers make a conscious effort to follow this practice during the transformation stage, not only to reward genuine achievement but also to ensure the organisation recognises that they are willing to give credit where it is due, rather than selfishly seeking all the plaudits themselves.

CASE STUDY 19 – PIZZA HUT: GALVANISING THE ORGANISATION
Jens Hofma

Jens Hofma has been CEO of Pizza Hut UK since 2009 when he was parachuted in to plug its losses by its owner at the time, Yum! Brands. Previously, Jens was MD of KFC Germany. Earlier on in his career, Jens worked for Nestlé and McKinsey and has an MBA from IMD, Switzerland.

The challenge – when I arrived at Pizza Hut UK the business had been in a decline for over a decade... Transactions were being eroded at a rate of 3–6% per annum... the chain had made losses for three years prior to my arrival... [and] successive management teams – as good as they were – had attempted to turn around a brand that was now perceived as being in terminal decline... Over the last two years (2013–15) the brand has experienced two successive years of strong sales and profit growth... I would highlight eight fundamental factors that have contributed to our recent turnaround:

1. **Understanding customer feelings** – when I arrived, there seemed to be no clear analysis of what the problem with the brand was... There were several opinions – all, in my view, unsubstantiated... Management had kept focusing on trying to drive visit frequency through fantastic marketing campaigns but some people believed that we weren't giving people enough value through discounts, whilst others believed our operational execution was too poor... My view, which crystallised pretty quickly, was that we had a *restaurant experience* that did not hold its own amongst its competitors... it

was not exciting: it was bland and functional... The root cause of our decline related to a total absence of experiential 'emotional takeaway' for the customer, exemplified through '80s brown decor, transactional service and uninspiring food... My views were confirmed by some deep-dive research we did that looked at how customers *felt* and how they would like to *feel*... Our (dwindling) customers felt consciously/unconsciously secure in a safe, predictable and unintimidating environment in which they could roam free as a family... but our research established that they would like to feel three things:

- *Uninhibited* – i.e. not bored; allowed to experiment and 'let go' in a safe environment
- *Embraced* – i.e. relaxed and welcomed; an extension of family
- *Light hearted* – i.e. tongue in cheek; having a fun time.

2. **Motivated combined team** – what I now needed to get the organisation to focus upon was creating a new experience that would address these customer desires... The team that I assembled to do this job was what I call a 'combined team': a mixture between long-timers and disruptive change leaders... What I encountered when I arrived were a huge number of people who had a remaining sense of pride and affection for the brand... They remembered and had a sense of mourning for past good times... I engaged these passionate long-timers by involving them, asking them: *How can we revive the brand? How can we make the good times come back? How can we get back what we had in the '80s?* ... I challenged our long-timers in the restaurants and the support centre to fight and stand up for what they wanted! ... I certainly did not take the view that people that had a great degree of affection and institutional memory were useless or solely to blame – I wanted them on my side... Indeed, I have promoted some long-timers to senior positions... These are combined with a few disruptive change leaders that have brought new perspectives and dimensions to the party...

3. **Symbolic behaviour** – one thing I did that reinforced what I wanted the organisation to do was to personally go 'back to the floor'... Many senior people think they can keep in touch with what is happening on the ground through 'dog and pony show' visits... I didn't want our solutions for the brand to be over-theoretical or conceptual... I needed to get up close with the customer and our teams through working a shift a week... At first I didn't tell anybody for three or four months: it was important for it not to be seen as

stage managed... It gave me an excellent insight into what worked and the psychology of our team... Really, my behaviour was inverting the pyramid – I was closing down distance by working at the point of impact... I still do a shift a month now – I think it not only helps me understand the business better but also signals the central importance of our customers and restaurant teams to the wider organisation...

4. **Authentic brand personality** – so where did we get to? After asking what we wanted the concept to be – based on our customer insight – we filtered out everything that had made it survive and iconic... From a product point of view, we revived or improved certain elements such as the salad bar, lunchtime buffet, ice-cream bar, stuffed crust pizza etc. ... Fundamentally, however, we returned to the true north of the brand: an American take on Pizza! ... Previously, the brand had gone off track, copying or imitating competitor brands such as Ask, Zizzi, PizzaExpress etc. ... it had become a poor follower, bland and ill defined... it had lost its personality and soul: our customers said that we lacked authenticity! ... What had set it apart in the past was its original DNA: **American Pizza in an informal, non-pretentious, exciting service environment**... This was the basis of our new concept development which – having trialled a new menu, décor and service-delivery system – saw enormous sales uplifts in the original pilot units...

5. **Improved operational capability** – but because you can't convert the whole estate overnight (we are only 30% done at present!) we needed to apply a twin-track approach of refreshing the proposition whilst simultaneously improving execution. It is no good having a great revived concept but no operational capability... To this end, we have improved our 'hard' training and development systems that focus on great standards, superb shift management and customer service excellence...

6. **Growth mentality** – at the same time, we have concentrated on getting our managers back into a growth mindset... Many of them had learnt to survive by complying in a declining business... We did three things here: invested in more labour, spent more on maintenance and released some of the controls that had held back our managers from experimenting and improving the offer on the ground... To give you one example, in one of our outlets we asked our team 'what is holding you back?' in key sessions... they told us that the company's obsession with customer feedback slip return targets was an inhibiter... also that queues around the buffet at the

lunchtime daypart were capping sales... By changing a few things (ergonomics and FOH/BOH communication), we significantly increased cover turns in this restaurant...

7. **Supportive ownership** – our transfer from corporate into private-equity ownership three years ago is another factor that has aided our revival... Our owners have balanced expectations: they knew that there was no silver bullet and that we needed patience and time... Now we don't have to obsess about defending quarterly earnings, we can take a three-to-four-year time horizon on the business... which has given us the space to address the fundamental problems in the brand...

8. **Moral responsibility** – the last factor I would cite that has contributed to our current turnaround is the sense of moral responsibility I and my management team feel for the business... We have nearly 10,000 people alongside us in this business, most of whom work damn hard, day in, day out, to make a success of this brand... People have invested a lot of their lives in the brand and they are relying on us to at least try to make the correct calls... We take this responsibility seriously – that is why many of the top team have stayed the course from the start of the turnaround process... Reviving this brand is not just a job – it is a worthwhile 'heroic mission', something that will enable us all to make our mark! ...

6.2 Sharpen Execution

The previous section highlighted how Revivers galvanise an organisation into action; but what should they generally aim to *achieve* first? The answer in our view is simple: they should devote a high level of energy and focus towards sharpening up their brand's executional capability. What do we mean by this? A principal characteristic of brands that have lost their way – due to loss in morale, lack of direction and lax management – is a decline in standards, accompanied (as previously mentioned) by people avoiding accountability through 'avoidance' behaviours. The Reviver needs to get a grip of the organisation by removing its excess fat, introducing clear KPIs, streamlining structures to provide alignment and insisting on the enforcement of high operational standards that will restore its sense of professional pride. Of course, Revivers will also need to refresh the brand's proposition by re-shaping it to fit external market needs (see Section 6.3 below); but this cannot be achieved unless the fundamental basics of the brand are in place first in order to give it breathing space to generate innovation and land change. This was the leaping in point for Steve

Easterbrook, the newly appointed CEO of McDonald's, and his Chief Administrative Officer, Peter Bensen, when they set out their turnaround plan for the company in May 2015:

> Easterbrook said: 'The first critical step of our operational growth-led plan is to **strengthen our effectiveness and efficiency** to drive faster and more customer-led decisions. We will **restructure** our business... Our new structure will be supported by **streamlined teams with fewer layers and less bureaucracy**, and our markets will be better organised around their growth drivers'... McDonald's Chief Administrative Officer, Pete Bensen, said: 'As we restructure our organisation and instil greater customer focus, **McDonald's turnaround** will be governed by **stronger financial discipline, faster decision making and clear management accountability**...'
>
> (Charity 2015b)

> McDonald's chief executive, Steve Easterbrook, has insisted that Monday's **turnaround plan details** represent just the first step in directional changes, with more to come. 'We have only been in place for two months,' Easterbrook said. 'I've been very clear that **my number one priority has been to address operational issues**. These are the initial steps. There's more to do and more to come...'
>
> (Charity 2015d)

Easterbrook was parachuted into the job to revive one of the largest food service concepts in the world, which had been experiencing successive like-for-like sales declines in key markets. Clearly, he believed that the first step in the organisation's salvation was to sharpen its operational delivery. So what are the must do and high-value activities that Revivers must facilitate during this process?

Execution Qualifiers

Essentially, Revivers have got to get a grip on the organisation through both 'hard control' and 'soft ideological' means:

◘ **Reshape architecture** – the first act of the Reviver during the process of sharpening up execution is to ensure that the architecture of the enterprise is fit for purpose. To this extent, they will pose a number of questions. How efficiently is the operational line organised geographically: are the regions, districts and clusters achieving efficient coverage with optimal spans of control? Would the enterprise be better served by segmenting the estate (around the principles of scale, core/non-core, market maturity, customer need etc.)? Are the core functions aligned with, and where necessary embedded in, the operational line? Is there a case for aggressive estate repositioning, exiting sub-optimal 'drag' units to concentrate efforts on a smaller, high-quality portfolio? Is the business model still relevant: do we need (more) conversions from managed to franchised or vice versa?

- **Refine KPIs and measures** – with regards to what is being measured by the organisation, the Reviver needs to ask a number of key questions. Are the right behaviours being encouraged by the current KPIs and incentives? Has the organisation prioritised the correct measures to drive assured outcomes (i.e. is there a focus on profit outputs rather than service/standards inputs)? Are the targets in place too soft (resulting in shirking) or too hard (resulting in poor morale)? Are the KPIs for the organisation cascaded appropriately? Most importantly, do front-line service providers have simple, well-understood SMART objectives that link to the organisation's strategic priorities?

- **Reinvigorate monitoring** – as stated, often organisations that have drifted into the revive category have not only lost their mojo, they have lost their sense of operational self-respect and pride. The Reviver must investigate and reinvigorate the monitoring procedures in the organisation by making sure that operational line PAPs (period activity planners) have sufficient planned and unannounced 'visits with a purpose' and the company has sufficient resource (i.e. compliance and audit) to undertake rigorous, deep-dive operational assessments.

- **'Reboot' values** – alongside these 'hard' controls, the Reviver will need to revisit the values of the organisation by asking the following questions: are the values of the organisation still relevant and consistent with what we are trying to achieve as an enterprise? Are the values widely disseminated, understood and modelled within the organisation? Are they shaping and guiding intentional and purposeful behaviours that add value for the organisation? If the answers to some of these questions are negative, the Reviver will need to reboot the values system of the organisation through communications, personal example and publically recognising great values-led behaviours. As discussed in the introduction, by their very nature, multi-unit food service brands require the expediting of multiple tasks, transactions and 'customer touches' that *cannot* be governed by tight central control. Values systems clearly stating 'the way we do business around here' are one of the main mechanisms that brand leaders can leverage to bind the organisation together with a sense of common purpose and self-regulating behaviour. If they have become outdated or fallen into abeyance, the Reviver must recharge the whole values process.

Execution Differentiators

But what do the best Revivers do in order to sharpen the execution of the organisation during the transformational change process?

- ◩ **Go big, go fast!** – the Reviver would do well to observe the dictum 'less haste, more speed' during the process of transforming the operational capability of the enterprise: missteps at this juncture could prove costly further on down the line. Re-organising territories once, only to revisit them again later, undermines continuity of relationships and momentum. However, we believe that once the Reviver has done his/her analysis, s/he should 'go big and fast' in ringing the changes. Why? The organisation will be expecting change and the Reviver must seize this window of opportunity to transform it into an entity that is entirely fit for purpose. Revivers must take this opportunity to draw a line in the sand and reinvigorate the enterprise through bold, decisive action. The principal question most brand members will be asking is 'how will any change affect me?' The Reviver must ensure that this question is answered for people quickly in order to remove any doubt or fear. On balance, it is expedient if the changes that s/he makes actually benefit the majority of the brand members – but where this isn't possible, s/he should ensure that (at the very least) the core group that will be charged with taking the organisation forwards is properly focused and energised.
- ◩ **Zone of tolerance** – this section (rightly) emphasises the need for the Reviver to assert a high degree of operational grip within the enterprise during the transformation process. But raising the bar on standards and focusing brand members on key objectives needn't come exclusively at the expense of crushing any sense of empowerment and self-expression in the organisation. The company now needs to be more agile – to shed its bureaucratic past – and brand members will need to be more proactive and flexible going forwards to respond to changing consumer needs. The fact that 'grip' has been

asserted should not interpreted as instituting a paralysing punishment regime! Revivers are careful to balance the requirement for control with the need for autonomy. Brand members need know where the zones of tolerance lie within the enterprise – in other words, when and where they can deviate from the brand standard if they are providing value-added customer solutions (through localisation and customisation of some elements of the marketing mix, for instance).

- ◘ **Showcase excellence** – in order for Revivers to demonstrate to the wider organisation 'what good looks like', they should not only publicly recognise exemplars of best practice but ensure that there are sufficient 'beacon units' in their estate that showcase operational excellence in action. These sites can act as training repositories but their principal function is to enable other brand members to 'see, touch and feel' what the organisation aspires to for all its units of operation. These beacons must not only shine through high FOH standards and service levels but also through outstanding BOH practices and procedures that can be learnt from and imitated by wider brand members.

CASE STUDY 20 – **TOBY CARVERY: TURNING IT AROUND**
Kevin Todd

Kevin Todd has led successful food service brands both in the UK and internationally. Widely acknowledged as one of the most successful brand leaders of his generation, Kevin is currently a non-executive director of a number of food service brands and companies in the UK.

Originally founded by Mike Sabin in [1976], Toby Carvery is one of the most-loved restaurant concepts in the UK. It has 400,000 Facebook followers, serves 21 million meals out of 150 restaurants and has one of the highest Net Promoter Scores in the UK food service industry... It is by far the leading carvery brand in the UK – the self-proclaimed 'Home of the Roast'! ... But it wasn't always so... back in the day, when I was appointed Director and General Manager, the brand that had *completely* lost its way... Sites were down to 600 meals per week at £10.50 spend per head! ... It was in a sorry state... restaurants were being churned in and out of the brand every year... it suffered from an identity crisis – it had tried to reverse falling volumes through a chameleon concept (grill during the week and carvery over the weekend) which flopped due to a lack of clarity and quality... It had also persisted in trying to satisfy two tribes, both hardened drinkers and restaurant users in order to optimise sales, completely failing to satisfy the needs of either cohort of guests... So how did we turn this desperate situation around?

- ◘ **'Skunk works'** – one of the first decisions we made was to set up a completely separate entity outside of the brand in the stables of a place called Hillfield Hall... Here we could think outside the box in a separate space and test out our ideas in a simulated environment (testing carving decks, ergonomic flows, new designs etc.)...
- ◘ **Blended expert team** – the turnaround team I assembled to populate this 'skunk works' included experienced internals (Ian Dunstall from Marketing; Sheelagh Pegg, Noel Darcey and Peter Leece from Operations; Karen Skingley from HR etc.) and expert externals (JRA, the interior design expert team; Deterministics, the throughput and capacity management experts; Roy Halstead Ass. Inc, the product development expert etc.)... They all offered different insights and perspectives. What we produced in the end was really an integrated team effort...
- ◘ **'Think big'** – what we did was bind this group together by giving them one major goal: we were going to produce a template/prototype carvery that would do 3,500 covers per week (almost seven times more than the current volumes!)... The team we assembled bought into this vision (a couple of members that couldn't quite get their heads around it were quickly let go from the team)... Did I think this was achievable? ... Based on our knowledge of the industry-leading brands – which had mainly grill-based menus – I knew that it was! ... Indeed, to get a paradigm shift in our thinking and a real focus and energy about the team we purposefully made it our goal to 'go after' and 'hurt' certain brands (and we did!)... Our goal was to create a category *killer* in this segment, which we also achieved...
- ◘ **Refined marketing mix** – 'accessible Indulgence' was the brand positioning bridge statement we came up with for the brand... It guided the team during its efforts to assemble a totally refined concept across the entire marketing mix... Our research told us that customers loved carveries but that they didn't like them in their current environments; they didn't feel at ease... so (in line with the new positioning) we revisited and tweaked the following:
  - Inviting *place* – we did away with the 'two rooms' design (bar

and restaurant) to make the restaurant a 'one building' concept with a 'one tribe' mentality... To signify that things had changed, we created an abundant interior with a multitude of British humorous pictures, also painting the exteriors of the new templates terracotta; this signified to the customer 'we are different now!'... We wanted people to apply their brakes or stop in their tracks to see and wonder what was happening – once we got people through the doors we knew they would come back time and again...

- Slick *processes* – with Determinstics' help, we tested and reformatted the carvery decks and queuing systems to increase throughputs; eventually we went with meat and vegetables on a single deck with sauces/gravies at another station... This speeded up the whole food-collection process, resulting in better cover turns... We also put more production capacity in the kitchen to produce the kinds of volumes that this new template would generate...

- Quality *product* – previous leadership of the brand had gone down a deskilling route, substituting fresh vegetables with frozen... We reversed this... We wanted to be known for our range, quality and generosity; differentiated from other carveries (both in and out-of-home) by our freshness and abundance (three roast meats and eight fresh vegetables)... Customers could load their plates and return for a second portion of fresh vegetables if they wished...

- EDLP *pricing* – in order to generate volume spikes in the past, the brand had used a 'hi-low' strategy (discounting, BOGOFFs, vouchers etc.)... Learning from Walmart at the time we completely swept this away with a transparent everyday low price (EDLP) strategy: we were determined to give more for less, not less for less! – 'Value, volume but with personality'... Carveries are a 'cook and hope' operation – you cook the food and hope customers are going to turn up... They are reliant on high volumes to maintain freshness: the higher the volume, the fresher the quality and the lower the wastage – BUT to put on a good display you have to put £250 worth of food on a Tuesday lunchtime... *so value to get volume is critical*! ... Being pragmatic (rather than gorging) on price would drive throughputs and maintain the quality and integrity of the offer...

- Motivated *people* – after we tested the new template (see below), we consciously changed the GMs of new investments and 'team tested' the FOH and BOH personnel... Why? ... Now the unit was switching over to the new 'one building' template, we thought it would be unfair for the existing GM to explain to his/her loyal drinkers why they couldn't come in now... A new GM, trained in the new 'Toby way' would find it easier to manage the transition from old to new (although we always made sure that displaced GMs got their own opportunity in other units further on down the line)... In terms of the house teams, we looked at who really engaged and got excited about the way things were going to be – we took them through how things would change... we engaged characters who used humour and bravado to entertain our guests... to teach carvers how to chat to the guests and provide personality to the experience – testing out connecting emotionally with guests when carvers are carving 1,200 meals during the Sunday lunch session! ... Generally, those team members that were uncomfortable with the new world would 'check out' themselves... Interestingly, staff turnover in the new sites (which had been approaching 110%) dropped to industry-leading levels of around 55–60%...

◘ **Prototype testing and roll-out** – the first three sites to be converted into the new prototype tripled or quadrupled their original turnovers, turning in stellar performances that they sustained over the longer term... We consciously kept the core estate away from the development estate as we rolled it out... But the net result for the brand was stunning... Within a few years we were signing three-year rolling contracts with farmers in Spain for their vegetables and became the largest purchasers in the UK of turkey and gammon...

What the revival of this brand came down to was a matter of **'Focus – Value, Volume with Personality!'** The creation of a solid brand positioning has enabled the business to maintain its focus over the years. This was bolstered by appointing successive brand champions as Director and General Manager who have the brand 'DNA' running through their veins, warding off stupid, short-termist, cost-engineering ideas that could take the brand back to the brink of oblivion! ...

6.3 Refresh Proposition

The Reviver has galvanised the organisation and sharpened execution but s/he must also refresh a brand proposition that has a diminishing customer base. Remaining customers will be delighted that the brand has tightened up its operational execution but do they truly need or love this brand? How does it benefit them in comparison to other food service options? In truth, Revivers can re-instil a sense of operational dynamism and optimistic momentum in the enterprise through their energy and passion but their efforts will founder unless they restore the brand's distinctiveness. To this extent they are in the same position as the Originator (see Chapter 2) – they must turn their attention to ensuring that their brand has a compelling culinary proposition with distinctive functional and emotional benefits that satisfy employee and customer needs, feelings and aspirations (resulting in attraction, loyalty and advocacy). Of course, unlike the Originator, they are not starting from scratch. They have inherited a brand that *had* a differentiated position in the market place with a vibrant personality and strong reputation. This has waned in the face of a fierce competitive onslaught and/or changing consumer behaviours. So what do they do now? This section will argue that the Reviver needs to go back to first principles with the brand, testing its salience and relevance, before instituting changes that – without compromising the brand's central essence – propel it back into category-leading status. But what actions *must* the Reviver take to achieve this objective and what *should* s/he do to optimise chances for success?

Refresh Qualifiers

Commentators who study, observe and write about company turnarounds are usually pretty prescriptive about what 'turnaround' leaders should do when reviving a moribund organisation. They generally advocate a sequential process of transformation involving the following stages: analyse (conduct a management review using activity-based costing, SWOT analysis and root failure causes analysis), plan (create a restructure and long-term strategic plan), do (seamlessly implement) and review (make incremental changes as necessary). They also point to the fact that there are various stages in turnarounds (acute needs, evaluation/assessment, restructuring, stabilisation, revitalisation and retrenchment) during which turnaround managers can deploy various strategies (selective shrinking, repositioning, replacement and/or renewal). Whilst these perspectives are extremely instructive and useful, our view is that there are four things that Revivers must do in order to refresh a brand's proposition:

- **Research trends and relevance** - the first thing that Revivers should do is conduct exhaustive quantitative and qualitative analysis into macro and micro culinary trends (see Chapter 2). Whilst doing so, they should ask the following questions with regards to both imitating and shaping: what are the happening brands in our segment doing that we're not? What can we imitate or bastardise immediately without compromising the integrity of our positioning? How can we shape the segment going forwards? How do we leverage developing consumer preferences and tastes to our own advantage? How can we restore our reputation for category leadership and innovation?

- **Recapture 'true north'** - in the first two chapters of this book we argued that successful food service brands start their lives with a focused position that either exploits or shapes consumer demand. Often it is the case that, far from needing dramatic repositioning, brands that have drifted off course from their original 'heroic mission' need to be put back on point. It is not that the original purpose of the brand has ceased to have any consumer franchise - the brand has, for a number of reasons, mislaid or forgotten what its true north was. Ad hoc, opportunistic behaviour has diluted the brand proposition, confusing both brand members and customers. What the Reviver must do is return the brand back to its founding vision of what it stood for and sought to achieve. This is not to say that the Reviver takes the brand back in time, remodelling the brand in the image of its original stores. No - what the Reviver must do is take the brand back to first principles, getting everyone in the organisation to understand its founding vision and spirit. From this vantage point, the organisation can successfully start to address how it improves both its marketing mix and distinctive employee/customer benefits.

- **Reinvigorate benefits** - having looked at nascent trends and re-established what the enterprise stands for, the Reviver now cheerleads functional and emotional enhancements to the brand. Chapter 2 detailed what these general benefits should be and achieve but, suffice it to say, certain employee and customer needs, feelings and aspirations have changed since the brand was founded. Bearing in mind the extant market insight, the Reviver must address the following questions: what enhancements to the brand can we (quickly) make now that will be of high perceived value to employees and customers (but low cost to us!)? Is the brand's value proposition (i.e. price, product quality, service and environment) imbalanced and, if so, which elements need fixing now? What changes can we make that – in accordance with the core purpose of this brand – will make our employees and customers love us again? What changes can we make to the marketing mix that will make us stand out from the crowd once again?

- **Review and roll-out** – inevitably, Revivers cannot take a scattergun approach to changing consumer-facing elements of the brand. Changes need to be rigorously piloted, trialled and measured in 'control' environments prior to roll-out. That is not to say that this process should be conducted in a slow, formulaic manner. We strongly urge Revivers to throw caution to the wind and go big with the remodelling of the marketing mix of a few key sites, albeit with slight iterations in each location. This will enable them to clarify what works – checking validity and replicability with employees and customers through use of the open-ended 'start, stop or continue?' question.

Refresh Differentiators

But what are the elements of refreshing the brand's proposition that enable the best Revivers to stand out from the rest?

- **Recapture excitement** – the first thing to say here is that Revivers will know they are succeeding if their changes recapture the original buzz and excitement of the brand. If employees are energised by the changes (resulting in higher retention and EOS scores) and customers react with enthusiasm (mirrored in higher NPS scores and spontaneous advocacy on social media sites) the Reviver is onto a winner. However, rather than declaring victory too soon, the Reviver will now engage in the same role as the Escalator and Evolver – rolling out changes across the estate, in a state of constant vigilance to incrementally improve and enhance the proposition. The brand might be saved for now, but the Reviver – or his/her successor – must focus upon scaling up the brand once more whilst persisting in continuous improvement activities.
- **Restore reputation** – the Reviver will also know whether or not they have been successful through analysing 'stakeholder narrative' concerning the brand. Suddenly the sinking ship has been transformed (to extend the metaphor) into a shiny new cruiser again. Customers, employees, suppliers, communities and the industry press have begun talking up, rather than talking down, the brand. Their

positivity in itself becomes a self-fulfilling prophecy, the brand – with humble but insightful stewardship – continues its journey back to 'front of mind', 'must use' status and desirability.

- ◘ **Futureproofed** – hopefully the changes that the Reviver has made to the brand will sustain its growth over the short to medium term. The question is, how can Revivers futureproof the organisation against any further calamities or reversals? This is fundamentally achieved by ensuring that the organisation is set up to be lean and agile enough to respond to future competitive threats and changes in consumer behaviour. Now that operational grip has been restored and the proposition has been refreshed, the Reviver's legacy should be a transformed organisation that can pre-empt any 'future shocks'. Cleaned of excessively bureaucratic behaviours and used to adapting to change, the organisation should – at least for the foreseeable future – be able to prosper in the turbulent external market.

CASE STUDY 21 – **REFRESHING THE PROPOSITION**
Philip Harrison

Philip Harrison is the founder–owner of the leading international leisure design company, Harrison Design. Since its foundation in 1990, this multi-award-winning organisation has delivered impactful, durable and profitable design-led solutions for some of the world's most famous leisure brands.

What are the main reasons behind successful brand overhauls? In my view – having been involved in many makeovers (most of which have been extremely successful) – I think there are five main drivers behind their success:

1. **Composite approach** – brand makeovers work best when leaders address every aspect of the business. In my experience, brands have usually lost touch and engagement with their guests at several levels: the service has drifted off, the product has become overly cost engineered and the environment lacks sparkle. The brand has in fact become a loose cannon, copying its competitors at every turn; in short, it has forgotten why exists or what it stands for! ... The best way of solving this malaise is to take a multi-faceted, composite approach that addresses all aspects of the marketing mix to get it back on track...

2. **Brand essence understanding** – but where should brand leaders start? What I would advocate – based on extensive experience and observation in this area – is to go back to the beginning. Very often the reasons why the brand was founded *still resonate today*. Often brand leaders – desperate to halt the downwards spiral – have resorted to copying other brands... they have not remained true to their own brand values... This has created confusion amongst both guests and staff: they no longer know what the brand stands for... To get back on track, brands often have to retrace their steps, realising that in order to thrive again they needn't throw the baby out with the bathwater... what they need to rediscover is where they came from and what their founding raison d'être was... Once this has been achieved, they can work on the nuances that will make it relevant in today's environment...

3. **Brand journey understanding** – in addition to understanding the original heart and soul of the brand, leaders would also be well advised to understand the journey that has got them to the point they have reached today – *what is the back catalogue of missteps? What is the archaeology of their present malaise?* Such an understanding will help brand leaders to understand both the scale of the problem and how they can approach the process of vigorous regeneration...

4. **Staged process mentality** – generally, the CEO or MD of the brand will have assembled a team to tackle the brand reinvention challenge. In many cases, this leader will be further ahead than their team in their understanding of scale of the problem and the radical solutions required to remedy the situation. Some team members will be highly sceptical and resistant to change; others will opt for pixie-dust patch-ups rather than (badly needed) transformational solutions... As designers, we often hold the client's hand by taking them on a journey to apply more radical solutions than they had ever envisaged... forging higher levels of trust over time as they begin to digest where we are taking them... After the first pilot we might have achieved 40% buy-in, but as the project snowballs in terms of success, these resistors often shed their prejudices and baggage and become our greatest advocates! ... The point I am making is that most transformational change in food service brands is a staged process where confidence and momentum builds over time rather than on the first day...

5. **Smart brand individuality** – the last point I would like to make applies to successful food service brands in general. There is a marked trend in this sector to seek local or so-called 'customised'

solutions. My view is this: people have a craving to use brands because brands convey trust through *consistently* addressing specific guest needs, feelings and aspirations. That is why they exist. The challenge for brand leaders is not necessarily to blend in with local environments but to seek to achieve a high degree of perceived individuality... If I take one major account we have worked for (one of the fastest-growing fast casual concepts in the world), they have no design manual... All their units are completely different in decorative terms, bar their distinctive stories on the wall and ethnic artwork... What we have done is match the décor to different relevant user groups: glamorous in up-market sites and grungy industrial in more off-beat locations... I always advocate looking at the geography of a site in its widest sense (i.e. internal dimensions, building and location) to make it look and appear authentic... The benefits of this are twofold: first, it allows the brand to constantly evolve and push the boundaries (a habit-forming device that guards against the laziness of formulaic standardisation); second, it enhances the guest experience (as they discover different nuances to their favourite brand) and motivates the management team (because they can see and operate something that looks different!)...

Further Thoughts

This chapter has analysed the role of the Reviver during the 'turnaround' transformation process of an ailing food service brand. The previous chapter (Chapter 5, 'Perish') detailed how brands can accelerate - full throttle! - into oblivion through incompetence, starvation and/or obsolescence; but we have argued here that brands can be reversed out of their (seemingly) intractable decline. How realistic is this position? The first thing to say is that many food service brands - once they begin the downward spiral - are almost impossible to rescue because they have passed a point of no return. They have been overrun and surpassed - they have become irrelevant. Secondly, the role of Reviver is an extremely difficult task, which few brand leaders have the requisite skills or attributes to fulfil. We argue that in order effect a turnaround, the Reviver needs to galvanise, sharpen and refresh the brand. This requires Revivers to possess what might seem to be a blend of contrasting characteristics: the ability to be both 'big picture' and detail orientated, both hands on and delegative and both a controller and a coach! Or to put it another way, the Reviver needs to exhibit exemplary leadership *and* management skills in order to achieve an effective brand turnaround. Do such people exist? Our case studies show that these animals do exist in the food service firmament, though they are few and far between. Because of their personality type – energetic, restless, courageous and 'adrenalised' – they rarely remain in organisations once they consider that their work is done. Revivers move on to different challenges involving 'big change' rather than staying around for the long, hard, evolutionary grind that now lies before the enterprise. The legacy of their efforts, however, remains like that of their close cousin the Originator – they become heroic figures in the brand's history, living proof that the brand should never contemplate or accept defeat!

CHAPTER 7   **Conclusion**

SEVEN

This book was prompted by a desire to explore and explain the behaviours, attributes and essential tasks of effective food service brand leaders. Why is this important at this time? It is quite evident to us and a number of other commentators that, as this book is being written in 2015, the UK is experiencing a race for space amongst a burgeoning number of branded food concepts. This excerpt, reporting on the sector's growth in September 2015, sums up the 'bull run' that is currently being experienced by the sector:

> CGA's Peach Market Growth Monitor reports net new openings of 1,770 restaurants in past 12 months: … the eating and drinking out market saw a net 1,770 new restaurants open in the last 12 months, according to latest data compiled for the new Market Growth Monitor from AlixPartners and CGA Peach. Branded food pubs saw a 9% growth in numbers – and the bulk of the overall growth in restaurants came from the, largely branded, chain restaurant market. … The suburbs, in particular, saw a marked 'move to food', with a 5.2% increase in those type of operations – not far behind the growth rate in urban centres. 'The figures from our first Market Growth Monitor illustrate that restaurant growth is genuinely a UK-wide story, with growth in many parts of the UK outstripping that of London,' said Paul Hemming, managing director, AlixPartners…
>
> (Charity 2015e)

These new openings of nascent and established brands, which are spreading out throughout the regions of the UK, are clearly meeting a consumer need for 'assured' out-of-home dining experiences (particularly in the fast casual dining segment of the market). But the question is, which brands will prosper and which ones will perish in the medium to long term either when the sector reaches over-capacity or when the economic tide turns? The answer to this – in our view – is largely down to brand stewardship. Successful brands can be launched only to wither on the vine through a lack of effective leadership through their transitionary phases.

But is that it? Is the secret to sustainable food service brands merely effective leadership through the various lifecycle stage transitions? Or are there common principles that apply to successful brands that effective leaders merely apply? It is certainly the view of many practitioners and academics that there are certain common denominators of food service brand success that have a positive impact. In addition, the narratives provided by many of the brand leaders in the case studies contained within these pages also point to converging characteristics of successful/sustainable food service brands. And what was this point of consensus? Quite simply, once the brand proposition has been proof-tested and found to be successful, the longevity of brands comes down to giving staff and customers their due, namely: **distinctive uplifting experiences**. Unlike FMCG environments, hospitality provides consumers with bundled experiences that stimulate the senses. The degree to which brand leaders design and perpetuate critical functional and emotional elements of experiential distinctiveness will ultimately determine the fate of the brand. Also, the presence of brand hardware (proposition, design, menu, site etc.) is nothing without its uplifting software: brand members with soul and personality that bring the brand to life in the eyes of the consumer.

This conclusion will, therefore, briefly reprise practitioner and academic perspectives regarding the origins of strong service brands, coupled with the position we outlined at the beginning of the book. It will then highlight the two major contributions of the book which are referenced in the title. First, the notion of critical transitions for effective brand leadership – the fact that different leadership approaches are required at different stages of a brand's development. Second – based upon the case study narratives of the brand leaders in this book – the core dimensions of sustainable food service brands, namely: to 'be different' (through several multi-faceted dimensions of providing distinctive uplifting experiences) and 'stay different' (maintaining experiential distinctiveness through melded teams and evolving the offer whilst maintaining the brand's core essence).

7.1 Reprise – Strong Brands

What are the main characteristics of strong brands? How do successful brands gain 'mindshare' advantage over their competitive set, engendering a holy-trinity payback of *loyalty*, *spontaneous advocacy* and *trial*? In our Introduction, we outlined the idiosyncratic nature of food service compared to FMCG brands, which included features such as: intangibility, service performance, heterogeneity, on-site production, customer involvement, perishability and the difficulties associated with evaluation. But how do strong brands rise to these challenges? To the academic high priest of service brand literature, Berry (2000), strong service brands constitute a 'valuable market offer' through: 'daring to be different' (defying convention), 'determining their own fame' (focusing on unserved market needs) and 'making an emotional connection' (seizing customer hearts through closeness, affection and trust). Other prominent academics operating in the service branding space advance the argument that strong brands are reliant on a 'focused position, consistency and values' (De Chernatony and Segal-Horn 2003).

In the food service domain, expert practitioners like Kroc (1977), Schultz (1998) and Meyer (2010) stress the importance of 'consistency and quality' (operational execution and locational choice), 'people who are informed and enthusiastic about brand' and the practice of 'enlightened hospitality' (when customers sense 'the other person is on your side'), respectively. Prominent food service academics like Muller (1998) highlight the importance of 'quality, service execution and an evocative image' whilst Jones and colleagues (2002) point to the necessity for strong brands to have a 'focused position, consistency and values'. Service excellence specialists such as Heskett and colleagues (1994) pinpoint the importance of 'internal service' determining 'external service' outcomes, whilst others highlight the importance of 'enlightened HRM' and high investment in key 'moments of truth' as providing brands with strong competitive advantage. Finally, leadership lifecycle commentators (such as Reynolds et al. 2007) make the argument that as organisations transition through different phases of growth, different leadership styles are required to keep them on an 'upward trajectory'.

But what are we to make out of all these analyses, findings and observations? The first thing to say is that there is a great deal of convergence between what practitioners and academics believe to be the antecedents of strong brands, with 'focus', 'quality' and 'consistency' being constantly referred to as fundamental building blocks. In addition, the people dimension is acknowledged as being vital within the service domain. This is a critical and inimitable source of competitive advantage to operators who can get it right during key moments of truth. The second thing to say is that, useful as these definitions are, they fail in our opinion to really bind the whole thing together. It is our view, as stated in the Introduction, that there is a universal *unifying definition* that encapsulates the essence of strong brands which can be expressed in the following model and definition:

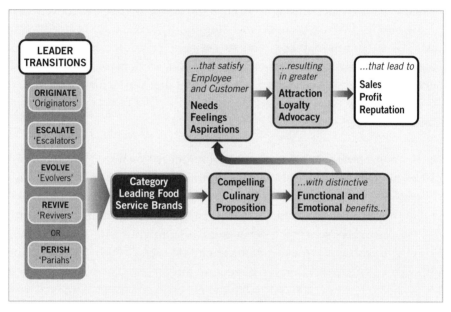

Figure 7 **Effective Brand Leadership Model**

> Category-leading food service brands are built around a compelling culinary proposition with distinctive functional and emotional benefits that satisfy the needs, feelings and aspirations of *both* employees and customers, resulting in greater attraction, loyalty and advocacy... (that in turn lead to growing sales, profit and reputation for the owner.)

This model combines *two* critical aspects of food service brands. First, it links leadership styles to a definition of brand success, whatever stage the brand is at during its lifecycle. In this sense, we believe that the factors underpinning brand strength are fairly immutable. Second, whilst stating that category-leading brands must have a sound foundation (i.e. a compelling culinary position), the framework suggests that their ultimate success rests upon the *simultaneous* satisfaction of the needs, feelings and aspirations of both employees and customers. In this sense, we do not see employee and customer satisfaction as binary – they are mutually interlinked and symbiotic. As we shall see, this position was endorsed by the case-study respondents of this book: prominent brand leaders who all stressed the importance of giving employees uplifting experiences so that, in turn, they would provide their customers with uplifting experiences! We will come back to this position after the next section.

7.2 Critical Leadership Transitions

A core theme of this book has been the nature and dimensions of effective brand leadership within food service contexts. Whilst we maintain that *what* brand leaders are aiming to achieve in order to create and sustain strong brands is relatively universal, the process of *how* they do it – due to various lifecycle stages – is not! What are these key differences in approach by which brand leaders are seeking to achieve admittedly the same outcome – sustainably strong brands within a highly competitive market place? Most importantly, what did the brand leaders interviewed for this book isolate as the key variables for success during these important transitional stages?

- ◻ **Originators** – in Chapter 2, we highlighted three core areas that Originators of food service brands need to concentrate upon in order to create a successful brand, namely: robustly *researching the gap*, carefully designing a *compelling concept* and purposefully constructing a *vibrant culture*. We argued that Originators in food service are often men or women with incredible zeal and determination who have learnt from painful previous failures and missteps; individuals on a heroic mission with an understandably – given the obstacles they need to overcome – high degree of autocratic charisma. Indeed, the one insight that is required to understand the underlying nature of successful Originators can be summarised as follows:

> Originators who invent successful brands *don't* start with an underlying profit motive or indeed a 'planned exit'... what they start with is a PASSION... a visceral mission to *make their mark!* ... successful brand originators intuitively understand that profit is the 'byproduct of innovation'... that 'creativity is the *leading* edge, profit the *trailing* edge'!
>
> (Tony Hughes on Originators, Case Study 2)

Problems for Originators lurk when the first thrust of the brand launch comes to an end and the brand requires systemisation for a successful scale roll-out. Often, due to their sense of heroic infallibility as 'founding fathers', Originators are loath to let go of any decision making. Their inability to accept that the brand – whilst retaining its core essence – must professionalise its processes and slaughter sacred cows that matter more to the Originator than the customer, means that brands can often founder at this point unless leader change is imposed or graciously acquiesced to by the creator of the brand.

- ◘ **Escalators** – following successful proof of concept, the next stage of the brand lifecycle is the process of scaling up that concept. In Chapter 3, we examined how so-called Escalators of the brand at this stage ensured a successful transition into a hyper-growth phase through *network acceleration*, *organisational systemisation* and *driving awareness*. We argued that some Originators *could* make the transition into this role if they possessed the right mindset and a sense of heightened self-awareness. However, in most cases, it is more likely that they will either be augmented or supplanted by professional managers who could rise to the challenge of driving a well-ordered push for market pre-eminence and category leadership, where both strong leadership *and* management skills would be required. Escalators must simultaneously preserve the core essence and DNA of the brand whilst organising and implementing robust systems that will ensure the brand stands the test of time. In order to achieve this objective, as Jillian McLean remarked in Case Study 7, Escalators need to create the right team around them:

> **'B-to-C' team** – whilst we have had a great team that has got us from A-to-B in our journey, through creation and start up, we have had to spend a lot of time recruiting people with roll-out skills and experience that can get us through the next stage... Our first phase of development was characterised by energy, passion and a 'can-do' attitude; this current phase requires more of a planning and organisational mindset (without undermining the brand essence)... In addition, we have had to be quite ruthless in making sure that business does not tail off in our original sites through distractions posed through openings elsewhere...
>
> (Jillian McLean, founder, Drake & Morgan, Case Study 7)

The process of growing a brand quickly at this stage is highly exhilarating and exciting for all those concerned. At some point, rapid roll out will slow down as successive micro-markets have been addressed. Now the Escalator must adjust to a new paradigm: that of patient incrementalism! Whether or not the Escalator has the patience or motivation to transition to a process of grinding it out is debatable; often, the next stage of development – that of evolution – is bequeathed to a leader that is more attuned to continuous improvement rather than adrenalised roll out.

■ **Evolvers** – having been rapidly rolled out to spatially pre-empt the competition, category-leading brands enter a slower cycle of roll-out growth. However, imposters and imitators will be doing their level best to 'steal their lunch'! At this stage, the brand must strive to keep ahead of the game through maintaining a state of healthy paranoia, as many of the case-study respondents argued. In Chapter 4, we argued that Brand leaders at this stage – whom we termed Evolvers – must focus on three areas, namely: ensuring the organisation has excellent *customer insight* systems to track changes in market demand, coupled with high levels of *organisational agility* and *implementation capability* to stay on-trend through continuously improving the offer. Unlike in FMCG goods contexts, however, food service leaders have a major advantage which Evolvers will actively leverage to their benefit:

> [Evolvers] use market research to *validate* but not necessarily *create*... [Unlike in FMCG goods, in] service hospitality, Evolvers can easily set up a trial in a unit and 'go see, touch, feel and hear'... in this sense they can act *quickly* on intuitive hunches garnered from a number of sources rather than voluminous data sets... Great Evolvers of brands spend a disproportionate amount of time getting into what I call the 'headspace' of their guests... and this can only be fully achieved through face-to-face contact and observation... In my view, effective Evolvers are adept at spotting opportunities in dayparts by *becoming more democratic*; attending to the different needs of customers at specific times and/or ensuring that different customer sets can coalesce (through product laddering, service fit, zoning and environmental management) at the same time...
>
> (Ian Dunstall, brands guru, Case Study 11)

The major issue that Evolvers face, in spite of their best efforts and due to the size and scale of the organisation, is the prospect of creeping, crippling bureaucracy that suffocates any form of lateral thinking or innovation. Also, because many brand members are new, there is a danger that they fail to understand its brand archaeology and core essence, which have been diluted or lost in the mists of time. It is at this point that the brand faces an inflection point that will either lead to terminal decline or, if it can heed a wake-up call, revival.

◻ **Perish** - having failed to evolve - its competitive set having caught up with and superseded it - the erstwhile category-leading brand is in severe jeopardy. But why does it finally disappear from the branded firmament? Chapter 5 outlined three major reasons why brands perish, including: *managerial incompetence, resource starvation* and/or *product obsolescence*. Often the three factors are tied together but - as the veteran US senior food service operator, Frank Steed, stated - one driver will accelerate the decline of any concept, whatever its original strength:

> **Convergence** – the biggest reason, in my view, why US food service brands have failed – particularly within the sit-down casual sector – is because they merged... that is to say, they all began to look and feel the same over time... the fast casual sector that has emerged over the past fifteen years, offering quicker, less expensive ways for consumers to get food, made full-service casual theme brands look outdated and irrelevant; places where the menus looked the same, the service was average and the environments unexciting... Brands in this segment of the market did not evolve... they did not work hard enough at setting themselves apart... there was no sense of differentiation or uniqueness...
>
> (Frank Steed, ex-CEO US brands, Case Study 14)

This so-called 'isometric convergence' within segments - where the same people are shuffled around the sector with the same advisors and contacts, applying the same old solutions to new problems - is a major threat that looms in the UK for certain segments of the food service market, particularly branded pub restaurants. When this issue is coupled with other issues such as egoist leaders, gorging owners and substantial underinvestment, it is easy to see why some brands – starved and unloved by both staff and customers – hurtle towards obscurity. There is a route to redemption and salvation, however, if – onto this burning platform – a Reviver is encouraged/allowed to stride and prosper.

- ◘ **Revivers** – is there a way back for brands that have lost their mojo and are careering towards extinction? In many cases, the answer is simply 'no'! A failing brand is usually trapped within a so-called 'spiral of doom', its talent having long since departed, the brand being left with a diminishing cohort of 'hard loyalist' customers. But it does have one attribute that brand leaders attempting to turnaround the business can leverage: a sense of fondness and warm nostalgia amongst remaining long-time staffers and lapsed users who can nostalgically recall the way things were and how the brand used to make them feel. In Chapter 6, we analysed the role of the turnaround specialist – whom we termed the Reviver – in reinvigorating a seemingly lost cause. We highlighted three areas that Revivers concentrated upon to reignite the brand, namely: *galvanising the organisation, sharpening up its execution* and *refreshing its brand proposition.* We argued that in a sense, the Reviver is similar in outlook and disposition to the Originator – somebody who is possessed with a sense of heroic mission who exhorts, co-opts and motivates brand members to achieve great things that they never thought were even remotely possible:

> **Motivated combined team** – … The team that I assembled to do this job was what I call a 'combined team': a mixture between long-timers and disruptive change leaders… I engaged these passionate long-timers by involving them, asking them: *How can we revive the brand? How can we make the good times come back? How can we get back what we had in the '80s?*
>
> (Jens Hofma, CEO, Pizza Hut, Case Study 19)

The Reviver re-instils confidence in the brand, usually by returning it to its founding principles that have been homogenised by previous leadership cadres. By refocusing brand members on the original core purpose, these courageous, energetic and restless individuals create a sense of higher purpose and meaning amongst their followers. At the same time, however, they make great efforts to contemporise the brand so that it meets current rather than past consumer needs, feelings and aspirations. When their work is done, Revivers – who become mythical figures in the brand's history – generally move on to another challenge. The brand now moves back into an incremental evolutionary mode and the Reviver seeks out other transformational opportunities that sate his/her need for fulfilment through 'cliff-hanger' challenges.

7.3 Be Different – Experiential Distinctiveness

The notion of brand leadership transitions formed the spine of this book, its central premise being different 'folks' (or at least approaches) for different brand 'strokes'! However, our original definition of successful food service brands conceived of a set of universal characteristics that apply to category-leading food service brands whatever their lifecycle positioning (see figures 1 and 2). In addition, there was a remarkable convergence between the narratives of our case-study respondents as to which factors underpin strong food service brands. What were these points of convergence?

◘ **Experiential distinctiveness** – distinctive uplifting experiences marked out great brands from average brands and were comprised of three inter-related parts:
  - **Distinctive brand positioning** (for all stakeholders and users)
  - **Distinctive functional benefits** (for staff and customers)
  - **Distinctive emotional benefits** (for staff and customers).

Taking the 'halo' component – experiential distinctiveness – what did our brand leaders actually say? Taking a selection of comments:

> Our mission is to 'lift people's spirits'...
>
> (Jamie Barber, founder, Cabana, Case Study 4)
>
> *Compelling concept* – the first thing we devoted ALL our energies to was creating a compelling concept with soul and personality; an iconic brand that served American-style fresh burgers 'done well' off a 'small and sweet menu' in individualistic restaurants that all had different, intriguing designs... We sought to provide 'consistently amazing and memorable experiences' so that people would spread the word and keep coming back! ... our passion [is

for] producing fantastic, quality hamburgers delivered by people with personality in highly desirable places...

(Tom Byng, founder and CEO, Byron, Case Study 9)

...we created a great experience and atmosphere for guests by employing people we wanted to work with who bought into the ethos of the brand...

(Russel Joffe, founder, Giraffe, Case Study 6)

...its point of difference at the time being a number of iconic design features... and great staff who generated a great atmosphere/customer experience (Antipodeans with a great service ethic)... [we are in the business – after all – of SELLING ATMOSPHERE!]...

(Sue and Paul Salisbury, co-founders,
Premium Country Dining Group, Case Study 10)

We had to restore the brand to its former glory – bad decisions (made on the basis of panic and confusion) had allowed it to drift away from its sweet spot... I was determined to 'redifferentiate' the brand – giving our guests an experience that could not be replicated elsewhere! ... It is my view that we are now in a white space that we can command... we are clear category leaders within a category of one... We are THE experiential brand!

(Karen Forester, CEO, TGI Friday's, Case Study 18)

...the root cause of our decline related to a total absence of experiential 'emotional takeaway' for the customer; exemplified through '80s brown decor, transactional service and uninspiring food...

(Jens Hofma, CEO, Pizza Hut, Case Study 19)

...we engaged characters who used humour and bravado to entertain our guests... to teach carvers how to chat to the guests and provide personality to the experience – testing out connecting emotionally with guests...

(Kevin Todd, ex-Director and General Manager,
Toby Restaurants, Case Study 20)

Time and again, when referring to creating, sustaining or reviving brands, brand leaders stressed the central importance of delivering *distinctive uplifting experiences* with *soul, personality, spirit* and *atmosphere*. Like us, these experts recognise the fact that, essentially, hospitality is about bringing service performance to life, making it tangible and enjoyable for all parties concerned. But how is this achieved?

As stated – experiential distinctiveness does not, according to our brand leaders, mysteriously arise from the ether! In fact, whether consciously or subconsciously, it is very carefully engineered and/or restored by brand leaders around three fundamentals: a distinctive *positioning* combined with distinctive *functional* and *emotional* benefits for both employees and customers. The features that were attributed to these three dimensions by our respondents will be considered in turn, below.

7.3.1 Distinctive Positioning

The leaping-in point for the brand leaders interviewed for this book was that successful brands had to, first, aspire to or reach category-leading status:

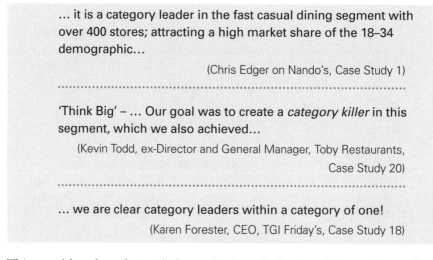

> … it is a category leader in the fast casual dining segment with over 400 stores; attracting a high market share of the 18–34 demographic…
>
> (Chris Edger on Nando's, Case Study 1)

> 'Think Big' – … Our goal was to create a *category killer* in this segment, which we also achieved…
>
> (Kevin Todd, ex-Director and General Manager, Toby Restaurants, Case Study 20)

> … we are clear category leaders within a category of one!
>
> (Karen Forester, CEO, TGI Friday's, Case Study 18)

This could only achieved through formulating/evolving a laser sharp culinary concept addressing a particular segment of the market:

> It has a clear and compelling culinary proposition: spicy chicken with attitude…
>
> (Chris Edger on Nando's, Case Study 1)

... substitute the 'value' steakhouse with a 'premium' steakhouse offer (there's always demand for a good steakhouse: think of Berni or Beefeater) – the trick is KISS (keep it simple stupid)...

(Tony Hughes, founder, Miller & Carter, Case Study 3)

[A] lifestyle brand based on world music and global food with a style of doing business where we wanted no barriers to how we did things... a new niche – something that people didn't even know they wanted... an all-day brand... with a world take on music, décor and food... the name 'Giraffe' embodied what we wanted to convey: tall, exotic, fun, global...

(Russel Joffe, founder, Giraffe, Case Study 6)

... its main influence was a quality restaurant bar with an Italian twist...

(Sue and Paul Salisbury, co-founders,
Premium Country Dining Group, Case Study 10)

'Home of the Roast'... 'Value, volume but with personality'...

(Kevin Todd, ex-Director and General Manager,
Toby Restaurants, Case Study 20)

... the first thing we devoted ALL our energies to was creating a compelling concept... an iconic brand that served American-style fresh burgers done well off a small and sweet menu...

(Tom Byng, founder and CEO, Byron, Case Study 9)

... Fundamentally, however, we returned to the true north of the brand: an American take on Pizza! ... What had set it apart in the past was its original DNA: American Pizza in an informal, non-pretentious, exciting service environment...

(Jens Hofma, CEO, Pizza Hut, Case Study 19)

Often, this is buttressed by a core 'bridging' statement addressing functional and emotional elements of the brand that would guide future decision-making:

> ... The functional and emotional positioning values of Miller &
> Carter were defined as 'simple luxury' – communicated as 'little
> black dress'; a clear and descriptive way of understanding the
> brand role... an essential element for every woman to own is a
> simple, elegant black dress that can be dressed up or down making
> it suitable for a wide range of occasions – always with style...
>
> (Tony Hughes, founder, Miller & Carter, Case Study 3)

> ... it was an enormously successful partnership that conceived
> and rolled out a brand which was framed around its guiding
> bridge statement of 'Stylish Self-Projection' (it addressed new
> moneyed consumers who wanted the brand to reflect and
> reinforce their perceived social standing)...
>
> (Tony Hughes, co-founder, Premium Country Dining Group, Case
> Study 10)

> ...'accessible Indulgence' was the brand positioning bridge
> statement...
>
> (Kevin Todd, ex-Director and General Manager,
> Toby Restaurants, Case Study 20)

And underpinned by a sound business model that would enable scalability:

> One of the main outcomes is that Nando's fulfils one of the main
> criteria of strong brands, namely: the ability to charge a price
> premium coupled with a tight operational model (due to casual
> self-serve nature of the service cycle)...
>
> (Chris Edger on Nando's, Case Study 1)

> The financial model is extremely stable: energy consumption and
> staff costs are reduced and the division of labour allows for the
> raising of productivity...
>
> (Misha Zelman, founder, Burger & Lobster, Case Study 4)

> Scalability – One thing I had learnt from my earlier ventures is that
> you must build a brand to be scalable from day one... we
> deliberately built small well-kitted out kitchens that would only
> take three people to operate – even in busy peak shifts – so that

> we didn't build unnecessary costs into the model (big kitchens
> encourage 'menu creep' and excessive manning)...
>
> (Jamie Barber, founder, Cabana, Case Study 4)
>
> ....
>
> However, the original [Berni] footprint concept of two restaurants,
> two bars and two menus had significant failings... First, it was
> inefficient in terms of overhead cost control and efficiency... We
> therefore evolved the structure: ONE RESTAURANT, ONE BAR,
> ONE MENU... This produced a significant R.O.I. for Whitbread...
>
> (Alan Jackson, ex-MD, Beefeater Restaurants, Case Study 17)

7.3.2 Distinctive Functional Benefits

Once a brand has got its base-line positioning right, effective brand leaders recognise that they must ensure that the 'foundation' hygiene factors of the brand are put in place. What does this mean? Fundamentally, food service brands need to construct/rectify lower-order experiential factors for both customers and staff before they connect emotionally. These are the so-called 'brand basics' and are absolutely vital props: their absence will undermine the brand's promise, reputation and allure for both customers and staff. But which distinctive functional benefits for both customers and staff did our brand leaders identify in the case studies?

Functional Benefits for Customers

Broadly, what the effective brand leaders said can be split into two categories – delivery of assured consistency and high perceived value in relation to the overall proposition (i.e. an equitable price/product trade-off). Firstly, let's look at consistency – this was conceived of in three ways:

◻ *Consistent product quality* – respondents expressed a strong belief that one of the most important functional factors underpinning strong food service brands was consistency of food quality. This is something that they universally recognised as one of the main drivers of their reputation amongst customers. Ensuring dishes were made to specification and served at the right temperature was regarded as a fundamental hygiene factor of food service brand strength. (This assured consistency of performance reduces risk for customers, which is one of the main reasons brands exist and is thus a major qualifier for brand success.)

> [We aim] to create a 'cult' of one dish and do our best to make it perfect... The quality of preparation of this dish is as close to ideal as possible... [We intend to] make a restaurant famous and popular by providing supreme quality of food preparation...
>
> (Misha Zelman, founder, Burger & Lobster, Case Study 4)

> ... Yes, the core strength of the brand is derived from obsessive attention to detail to the core product (that we don't undermine by 'trading on price')...
>
> (Berry Casey, founder, Haché, Case Study 5)

> ... *Quality Product* – previous leadership of the brand had gone down a deskilling route, substituting fresh vegetables with frozen... We reversed this... We wanted to be known for our range, quality and generosity...
>
> (Kevin Todd, ex-Director and General Manager,
> Toby Restaurants, Case Study 20)

◘ *Consistent service* – alongside consistent food quality, the effective brand leaders interviewed for this book highlighted the importance of having a chain of service in place that was *clearly* understood by both staff and customers. In addition, they highlighted the importance of service delivery systems matching the positioning of the brand and expectations of the end user with regards to speed, 'touches' and execution (whether in full, fast casual, buffet or 'bar order, runner' service contexts):

> Robust service platform – ... Working with Pragma (a consultancy specialising in service delivery), we have simplified the customer service model by reducing the number of 'touch points' within the customer journey... this simplification will lead to greater consistency of execution from our teams and clarity of understanding from our customers as we move forwards...
>
> (Jillian McLean, founder, Drake & Morgan, Case Study 7)

◘ *Consistent standards and cleanliness* – alongside the fundamental requirements for consistent food quality and service, effective brand leaders stressed the importance – particularly given their food service context – of exemplary levels of hygiene and organisation, both BOH and FOH. Ensuring that their units 'shone' and their toilet facilities sparkled at all times was recognised as a matter of key importance, not only from a legal and environmental health viewpoint but also to customer perceptions of the brand:

> Improving standards and execution – In parallel with this we had to raise our standards: frankly our restaurants were dirty... How did we do this? ... First, we scrubbed everything until it shone and mended things that were broken... Second, we introduced operational 'deep dive' inspections where we thoroughly scrutinise cleanliness and test the knowledge/skills of all our team to ensure units are 'ready'...
>
> (Karen Forester, CEO, TGI Friday's, Case Study 18)

> In order to 'internally franchise' the store, we tightened up the manuals and specifications... also introducing rigorous operations evaluation procedures (rigorous standards audits)...
>
> (Andrew Emmerson, ex-MD, Millie's, Case Study 8)

The second category of case-study respondent remarks was perceived value – this is the customers' belief that they are receiving good value for money in relation to the overall food service experience (product, environment and service), whatever the daypart, occasion or timeslot. Time and again, effective brand leaders highlighted the fact that their branded offer must achieve realistic pricing balance to drive footfall, recognising the fundamental perishability of their branded food service offers:

> The recession was weathered as we offered a low spend per head in chic surroundings...
>
> (Berry Casey, founder, Haché, Case Study 5)

> ... creating an affordable lifestyle brand...
>
> (Russel Joffe, founder, Giraffe, Case Study 6)

> [Berni] offered a known product at a known price and – most important to a country still steeped in class structure – it

introduced casual, relaxed dining atmosphere for 'ordinary people' – all on the base attributes of a multi-site branded *product with – importantly – no surprises... real value for money*! ...

(Alan Jackson, ex-MD, Beefeater Restaurants, Case Study 17)

EDLP *pricing* – in order to generate volume spikes in the past, the brand had used a 'hi-low' strategy (discounting, BOGOFFs, vouchers etc.)... Learning from Walmart at the time we completely swept this away with a transparent everyday low price (EDLP) strategy: we were determined to give more for less, not less for less! – 'Value, volume but with personality'... Carveries are a 'cook and hope' operation – you cook the food and hope customers are going to turn up... They are reliant on high volumes to maintain freshness: the higher the volume, the fresher the quality and the lower the wastage – BUT to put on a good display you have to put £250 worth of food on a Tuesday lunchtime... *so value to get volume is critical*! ... Being pragmatic (rather than gorging) on price would drive throughputs and maintain the quality and integrity of the offer...

(Kevin Todd, ex-Director and General Manager,
Toby Restaurants, Case Study 20)

Functional Benefits for Employees

In addition to fulfilling basic 'entry level' needs for customers, the brand leaders interviewed for this book also recognised the importance of addressing extrinsic motivators for their employees. Standard motivational theory stresses the importance of firms addressing basic hygiene factors for staff if 'higher order' intrinsic satisfiers are to be successful. Put simply, unless organisations get the basics right to address fundamental needs (i.e. fair reward, good working conditions, relative job security and enough resources to do the job) they are unlikely to cut through with supplementary emotional motivators that seek to address feelings and aspirations. But what functional benefits did the respondents cite? In addition to the obvious extrinsic factors highlighted above, many respondents mentioned the importance of reward within the context of generating hospitality excellence. This is unsurprising given the arduous and unsociable nature of the work; but it is generally addressed woefully across the sector in both the UK and US! What dimensions of reward did they cite?

◻ *Fair pay and benefits* – hospitality suffers from a poor reputation as a low-paid, low-skilled, low-barrier-to-entry profession that many people (such as migrants, youngsters and women requiring part-time work) enter not because they *want* to but because they have constrained choices (such as a lack of skills for higher-value jobs in other sectors). In the UK, the hospitality sector (unlike retail) has low levels of collective organisation and (some) employers are perceived as having exploited their labour through subsidising wages through tips and/or imposing zero-hours contracts which offer little security concerning regular hours and income flow. In time, a National Living Wage for over-25s coming into full force in 2020 might make the sector more attractive relative to other professions (unless many operators unscrupulously aim to employ a higher proportion of under-25s!). However, the respondents in this book were the first to recognise that, in order to gain some semblance of competitive advantage in the external labour market (during times of stellar sector growth and 'full' employment), they had to offer higher rates of basic pay and better benefits (holidays, shift drinks/meals, uniform allowances, sick pay etc.) than their competitive set – particularly for kitchen staff, an area in which, due to massive skills shortages, a 'war for talent' raged between operators:

> Employee benefits... it provides market-leading levels of pay and benefits...
>
> (Chris Edger on Nando's, Case Study 1)

> ... we really look after our people: we need to win in the Thai labour market! Our kitchen staff are on good pay and benefits...
>
> (Andy Laurillard, founder, Giggling Squid, Case Study 5)

> We also insisted that the kitchen was organised on a brigade system and that there were salaried staff front and back of house for attraction/retention purposes... Also the fact that the GM was being paid properly meant that s/he could live off-site...
>
> (Sue and Paul Salisbury, co-founders,
> Premium Country Dining Group, Case Study 10)

■ *Transparent incentives* – in addition to fair pay and benefits (that are proportionate to the work required and geographical location of the premises), there was a view amongst the effective brand leaders in the case studies that incentives should be spread widely and deeply throughout their organisations. This was not just the case with regards to the transparent sharing of tips but also the spread of share options and communication of bonuses:

> Also BOH and FOH share the rewards – in particular, tipping...
>
> (Andy Laurillard, founder, Giggling Squid, Case Study 5)
>
> ....
>
> The benefits of this were that managers became highly business literate and really tuned into any incentives that were running at any time... They were completely on top of the figures and their weekly and quarterly incentive/bonus progress, and so could communicate immediately to their store teams! ...
>
> (Andrew Emmerson, ex-MD, Millie's, Case Study 8)

■ *Equitable franchisee returns* – in franchised environments (which account for a fair proportion of UK hospitality) a couple of respondents with deep knowledge of the terrain stressed the importance of 'mutuality' – especially with regards to the division of profit. Franchisor 'gorging' (i.e. a disproportionate retention of income/profit) was viewed as harmful short-termism that would do huge damage to the brand:

> One further thought I would add is that given the transitory nature of much franchisor management, it is important that operational transformation is led by leaders with credibility who really monitor and care about franchisee profit... winning franchisors make good sustainable profit rather than bad short-termist gains...
>
> (Patricia Thomas, ex-Executive Director Operations,
> Domino's Pizza, Case Study 13)

7.3.3 Distinctive Emotional Benefits

The construction of a robust positioning and the ability to fulfil basic functional needs is a critical requirement of branded organisations; but what sets great brands apart from the rest is their ability to stimulate positive feelings and high levels of emotional attachment from both staff and customers. But which group comes first? It is our view, endorsed by the brand leaders featured in this book, that companies who generate significant emotional benefit for their employees will simultaneously gain a payback derived from the transferred emotional benefit for their customers (attraction, loyalty and advocacy):

> ... hiring, developing, motivating and retaining great service personalities lies at the heart of this brand... something that most of our competitors will always struggle to replicate!
>
> ... the one thing that we must never lose sight of again is that Friday's provides a high-end emotional experience... we don't really need to advertise... our guests are our raving advocates, departing with fantastic memories... it is the people factor in this brand that counts most...
>
> (Karen Forester, CEO, TGI Friday's, Case Study 18)

> In its citation for being the Best Large Company to work for in the UK in 2014, the company was recognised for outstanding engagement scores, low levels of staff turnover (relative to the rest of the sector), innovative development/progression programmes and industry-leading customer satisfaction scores. Clearly, the 'Nando's way' really resonates with employees, who reciprocate the care they receive from the company by caring about their customers...
>
> (Chris Edger on Nando's, Case Study 1)

> Thus, we introduced a new culture within a culture within M&B... motivated service personalities that were focussed on giving customers great experiences...
>
> (Sue and Paul Salisbury, co-founders, Premium Country Dining Group, Case Study 10)

Brand leaders in this book were quite clear: **engage your staff and you stand a high likelihood of engaging your customers**. Ensure your staff are having a fulfilling experience and, in all probability, your customers will have one too! But what distinctive emotional benefits did the respondents cite as being particularly important with regards to animating both staff and customers?

Distinctive Emotional Benefits for Employees

Brand Leaders in this book referred to a number of approaches they deployed to engender what Meyer (2010) terms 'enlightened hospitality' or de Chernatony calls a 'service personality'. But which ones were recurrent, regarded as 'must do's' – providing real tangible emotional benefit and distinctive uplifting experience to employees?

◘ *Family values* – the effective brand leaders interviewed for this book spoke fondly about their brands, often referring to them as a family with a defined set of values which protected and reinforced their sense of identity. Recognising that members of the brand 'tribe' could not carry manuals around with them to tell them how to act at all times, they sought to bind people in through a compelling 'ideology' that outlined some simple rules concerning the 'way we do things around here' – particularly in relation to the way 'we interact with one another and with our customers':

> 'Nando's is not just about the chicken. It's never been about the chicken. It's about the people who make the chicken... inspired by our adventurous spirit and values of pride, passion, courage, integrity and family...' Their sense of fun extends to changing the names of some positions (e.g. HR Director to Mother Hen, Transport Manager to Poultry in Motion)...
>
> (Chris Edger on Nando's, Case Study 1)

> ... how have we ensured that our service and environment are distinctive from canteen and better burger concepts that have challenged us over the past ten years? ... our philosophy is 'j'aime Haché, j'aime la vie' ('love Haché, love life'). We are in the business of *making people happy* – both staff and customers...
>
> (Berry Casey, founder, Haché, Case Study 5)

> ... we have strong values that are understood and bought into by all of our people top to bottom... cooperate – we stress cooperation as a cornerstone of the brand; highly necessary when you are refining and rolling out a new concept... share the work – hospitality is hard work, made easier if everybody pitches in to do whatever is required to delight customers...
>
> (Andy Laurillard, founder, Giggling Squid, Case Study 5)

> Supporting Values – Underpinning the company... you need a guiding compass for behaviours that keeps people on message and on track... common values... intended to create and drive intentional and purposeful behaviours... these should be woven into communications and KPIs to reinforce and shape actions... Evolving organisations need this glue so that brand members do not forget what the brand is all about! ...
>
> (Vanessa Hall, CEO, YO! Sushi, Case Study 12)

◘ *Symbolism and inspirational stories* - accompanying these strong values, effective brand leaders were acutely aware that they also had to illuminate the brand through metaphor and vivid imagery rather than bland rationalism. In order to tap into their brand members' psyches and create feelings of belonging/attachment, they worked hard to *create meaning* though stories and evocative symbolism:

> Our mission is to 'lift people's spirits', 'blowing them away with taste' through 'transporting them to Brazil' – we work hard to connect people (staff and customers) to the brand... our Cabana cookbook has sold 60,000 copies... It's really important that our employees understand our story and culture... buy into and exemplify the brand and we have taken a number of them on trips out to Brazil to really feel and touch the culture we're aspiring to replicate...
>
> (Jamie Barber, founder, Cabana, Case Study 4)

> ... particularly our philosophy of how we wanted to do business – *why we come to work every-day... We often said 'we happen to be in the people business serving food!'*... We lived the brand every day and this reflected what our teams were doing and this created *memories and stories* which made our customers come more often...
>
> (Russel Joffe, founder, Giraffe, Case Study 6)

> Symbolic Behaviour – One thing I did that reinforced what I wanted the organisation to do was to personally 'go back to the floor'... I didn't want our solutions for the brand to be over-theoretical or conceptual... Really, my behaviour was 'inverting the pyramid' – I was closing down distance by working at the

> point of impact... but [it] also signal[led] the central importance of our customers and restaurant teams to the wider organisation...
>
> (Jens Hofma, CEO, Pizza Hut, Case Study 19)

☐ *Personal communication* – in addition to closing down psychological distance between staff and the brand, effective brand leaders also sought to close down physical distance between themselves and their front-line teams through direct, face-to-face communication where they could explain the 'why', 'what' and 'how' to brand members:

> Also we were highly visible founders... interacting with staff and customers... finding out what they wanted... aligning common goals... communicating the message...
>
> (Russel Joffe, founder, Giraffe, Case Study 6)
>
> Coming into the role I decided that I would spend the first 100 days visiting 100 stores to 'watch and listen'... I started to work on our relationships with our franchisees by having informal meals and drinks with many of them, 'bringing them back into balance' (overcoming objections and problem raising) by asking about *how* they had got here today – listening to their stories, which almost served as a conscious reminder to them *why* what they were doing was important... We also set up regular calendar communications events which were designed to inform franchisees directly what we were doing, seeking their buy-in to changes...
>
> (Patricia Thomas, ex-Operations Director, Domino's Pizza,
Case Study 13)

☐ *Meaningful recognition and development* – understanding the importance of relative social standing to humans (i.e. the self-esteem people derive from their perceived social status/achievement), effective brand leaders were also consummate experts at shaping and deploying tangible forms of recognition for brand members that were designed to draw acclamation from peers, friends and family:

> [Millie's] had been led by a formidably talented husband and wife team who inculcated great values into the brand... they had

created a great environment for employees, creating a 'fun vibe' through recognition (regular communications, annual conference, incentives and bonuses; even birthday 'holiday' days off)... this rubbed off externally on customers: they felt good about using Millie's... they could see that the staff were enjoying themselves...

(Andrew Emmerson, ex-MD, Millie's, Case Study 8)

... But the starting point was always the team – they were the brand experience – they were the defining personality of the brand! ... We could fix the product and the environment; it was the team we had to start with first... How did we do this? ... [We introduced] a programme called 'Earn Your Stripes' where teamers had to achieve certification... then were recognised at graduation awards ceremonies... For me this marked the symbolic rebirth of the company and was the start of the turnaround... It restored a sense of team aspiration and buzz which translated into providing far better emotional service and higher sales/profits... the Executive Team goes out on site visits at peak sessions to 'catch and reward people doing great things!'... we retrain and recertify all our team every year to make sure that they have the right 'fit' (i.e. will and skill) to do their jobs...

(Karen Forester, CEO, TGI Friday's, Case Study 18)

◻ *Personality-based selection* – another form of emotional benefit highlighted by brand leaders was the rigorous and purposeful selection of brand members with authentic service personalities (i.e. people who get a thrill out of making customers happy). The advantages of selecting for attitude and personality are twofold: *first*, such employees 'brought the brand alive' in the eyes of the customer and, *second*, this hiring strategy was believed to create team harmony through a strong sense of purpose and shared values:

... we now have a much greater understanding of the type of people that we prefer – *attitude is so much more important that skills and experience...*

(Andy Laurillard, founder, Giggling Squid, Case Study 5)

Motivated *People* – ... In terms of the house teams, we looked at who really engaged and got excited about the way things were

> going to be – we took them through how things would change... Generally those that were uncomfortable with the new world would 'check out' themselves... Interestingly – staff turnover in the new sites (which had been approaching 110%) dropped to industry-leading levels of around 55–60%...
>
> (Kevin Todd, ex-Director and General Manager, Toby Restaurants, Case Study 20)

◻ *Autonomy and self-expression* – most of the brand leaders interviewed for the book believed in the concept of staff having a degree of 'flexibility within a fixed frame' not only because it enabled them to be more agile and responsive to customer requests (important because needs and expectations are rarely homogenous across different customer clusters) but also because it motivated them – granting them a degree of influence and self-expression within their local environments:

> ... for us it was about giving freedom to our people to express themselves; giving them wider barriers...
>
> (Russel Joffe, founder, Giraffe, Case Study 6)

> ... We did three things here: invested in more labour, spent more on maintenance and released some of the controls that had held back our managers from experimenting and improving the offer on the ground... To give you one example, in one of our outlets we asked our team 'what is holding you back?' in key sessions... they told us that the company's obsession with customer feedback slip return targets was an inhibiter... also that queues around the buffet at the lunchtime daypart were capping sales... [B]y changing a few things (ergonomics and FOH/BOH communication) we significantly increased cover turns in this restaurant...
>
> (Jens Hofma, CEO, Pizza Hut, Case Study 19)

◻ *Motivational design* – an increasing trend for food service brands to localise and individualise their local offer and design (perhaps adopting an 80–20 fixed-fluid template) also had the by-product of creating emotional buy-in and commitment from brand members who could feel a sense of pride and ownership about 'their' (slightly) customised unit:

> Smart brand individuality – ... People have a craving to use brands because brands convey trust through *consistently* addressing specific guest needs, feelings and aspirations. That is why they exist. The challenge for brand leaders is not necessarily to blend in with local environments but to seek to achieve a high degree of perceived individuality... it enhances the guest experience (as they discover different nuances to their favourite brand) and motivates the management team (because they can see and operate something that looks different!)...
>
> (Philip Harrison, founder, Harrison Design, Case Study 21)

Distinctive Emotional Benefits for Customers

Our respondent brand leaders saw the fostering of some or all of the emotional benefits for employees outlined in the section above as critical for creating experiential distinctiveness for brand guests. Their view was that creating a positive, fun and exciting environment for staff would stimulate enthusiastic service behaviour during critical 'moments of truth' with customers (the so-called 'emotional contagion' effect). They expressed a strong belief in creating vibrant 'people service' cultures which would 'personify' their brands – a form of inimitable competitive advantage that would create distinctive emotional benefits for their customers, who would then become their raving adherents and advocates. But in addition to citing memorable service encounters as a distinctive benefit for customers, what other benefits did brand leaders believe were required by guests at every stage of the brand lifecycle?

◻ *Memorable service encounters* – according to the brand leaders' narratives in this book, the most important emotional benefit that customers can receive from food service brands is a feeling of warmth and happiness generated through highly satisfying service encounters with pleasant, proactive and knowledgeable staff. Often, food service customers depart from premises with little other than memories. Great service (exemplified through personality, execution and rapid rectification), creates a great experience, leaving positive indelible memories:

> ...'First three feet' and 'bookending' – Memorable customer experiences that are delivered in what I call the '*first three feet*' and 'bookends' of the brand... A brand can have the greatest

design and product but it will come to nothing unless customers experience outstanding service at the 'point of impact'... this 'first three feet' is the moment of truth for any food service brand... the personality of the brand is defined not only by its functional aspects but also its emotional appeal, which is delivered – in large part – by happy, proactive and responsive front-line service providers... What ensures that companies excel in the first three feet? Simple – in hospitality, people *are* the brand in cultures which are built around internal and external customer excellence; a real desire to identify and satisfy differing customer needs, feelings and aspirations in the first three feet throughout the whole chain of service! ... BUT especially during the first impressions and the last impressions, *bookending* the experience... ensuring that three different people say 'hello!' or 'welcome!' and on departure three different people say 'thank you!' or 'see you soon'... bookending – three 'hellos!' and three 'goodbyes!'... as the old adage goes, 'you never get a second chance to make a first impression and last impressions last for an awfully long time!' This is particularly the case in hospitality where patrons often depart with little other than memories...

(Tony Hughes on Originators, Case Study 2)

◻ *Sensual stimulation* – in addition, the effective brand leaders interviewed for this book expressed the strong view that great experiences within hospitality occurred when all the sensory cues (i.e. smell, touch, see, hear, feel etc.) were aligned by the brand to positively stimulate and animate customers' perceptions of their visit. Often customers will make conscious and subconscious judgements of their food service experience. Great brands attract and retain customers in through 'locking in' sensory benefits that appeal to their customers' sub-conscious – making them intuitively feel that 'this is a great place to visit for this occasion!':

In addition, the tailored design of each store, high level of 'customer release/involvement' during the 'casual-style' chain of service and vivid sensory cues (sight: fiery orange/red colours; smell: 'spices'; sound: 'busy Portuguese town'; touch: sticky fingers; and taste: 'spices dancing on your tongue') make a visit to Nando's a memorable experience.

(Chris Edger on Nando's, Case Study 1)

Idiosyncratic brand icons – one thing that stands out about successful food service brands is some of their idiosyncratic features; that is to say, they have a number of key iconic 'artefacts or customs' that mark them out from the crowd... These icons can be expressed in design, culinary or service delivery terms... the fact is they 'distinguish' the brand from its competitive set, enduring throughout any changes that might occur in later years...

(Tony Hughes on Originators, Case Study 2)

Our mission is to 'lift people's spirits', 'blowing them away with taste'...

(Jamie Barber, founder, Cabana, Case Study 4)

TGI Friday's had been famous for giving great emotional experiences to its guests... it was renowned for its 'big personality': the fun, release and exuberance of its team; the boldness and generosity of its food; the flair and excitement of its bars.

(Karen Forester, CEO, TGI Friday's, Case Study 18)

■ *Loved loyals* – another significant emotional benefit offered by brands to customers, which our brand leaders deemed particularly significant, was the level of special attention and reward they lavish upon their loyal customers, rather than squandering goodwill and resources by chasing promiscuous, bargain-hunting 'switchers':

We have an incredibly loyal following who we reward through our Société Haché loyalty card and by putting on different specials every month ('vive le difference'!).

(Berry Casey, founder, Haché, Case Study 5)

Reward 'loyals' – ... the Byron Burger Club has grown from strength to strength and we continue to ramp up the rewards we provide to the more than 90k members of the Byron Burger Club – our most loyal customers... We want to ensure we offer these guys treats or enhanced experiences (such as interesting club events, one-off cook-off nights that enhance our 'burger expert' credibility)...

(Tom Byng, founder and CEO, Byron, Case Study 9)

■ ***Sense of community and affiliation*** - coupled with the rewards they gave to loyals - an expression of deep appreciation for their frequency of patronage - our brand leaders also stressed the importance of creating a sense of affiliation and community amongst their customers both inside and outside their units. Hospitality experiences are not solely framed by brand–customer relations; due to 'simultaneous coalescence', they are also affected (either positively or negatively) by customer–customer relations and interaction. The degree to which brands can create strong bonds and positive social interaction between users was seen by brand leaders as presenting mutual benefits to both the brand and customers themselves:

> ... and emotionally – customers feel Nando's provides 'warmth, irreverence, a social extension, stress relief, guilt-removing properties, friendly staff and good company'...
>
> (Chris Edger on Nando's, Case Study 1)

> The ambience and décor of our restaurants means that we are set apart from 'canteen lookalikes' – it is a place where people like coming to work and couples and friends like to socialise...
>
> (Berry Casey, founder, Haché, Case Study 5)

> *Leverage social media* – in addition to all of this we now dedicate resources to managing our social-media communities... they are the new and fresh voice of Byron and create stimulating conversations... indeed, we've had situations where we've been able to solve customer issues out immediately, live on Twitter... It's my view that the spontaneous feedback we get through social media is a great barometer of how we are doing as a brand: it provides a quick/easy way to get feedback; and because a lot of the rich narrative isn't necessarily directed at us (we are merely 'eavesdropping' on conversations) it has a higher degree of 'realness and authenticity'...
>
> (Tom Byng, founder and CEO, Byron, Case Study 9)

> Inviting *place* – we did away with the 'two rooms' design (bar and restaurant) to make the restaurant a 'one building' concept with a 'one tribe' mentality...
>
> (Kevin Todd, ex-Director and General Manager, Toby Restaurants, Case Study 20)

Outcomes of Distinctive Positioning and Benefits

But what are the outcomes of both fashioning a distinctive positioning and the benefits, functional and emotional, outlined above? What do brands get if they create uplifting experiences for their staff and customers? There are two things to say here. *First* – as the brand leaders stressed themselves (see below) – the success of a brand rests not only upon its experiential distinctiveness today (*to be different*); it is also contingent on its capacity to retain its experiential distinctiveness over time (*to stay different*). To this extent, brand leaders must keep supplementing, augmenting and tweaking their brand's benefits so that it remains sufficiently differentiated from its competitive set. *Second*, there was a high degree of consensus among our brand leaders that providing distinctive functional and emotional benefits to staff and customers – within the parameters of a focused, differentiated branded proposition – had a number of positive consequences. What were they perceived to be? *On the staff side*: lower turnover, higher engagement, higher productivity, better statutory health and hygiene scores etc. *On the customer side*: higher visit frequency, higher customer satisfaction scores and greater spends per head etc. In some cases, though not all, these outcomes translated into higher sales, margins and profit. We use Karen Forester's summary of the outcomes of her turnaround at TGI Friday's (2007–15) as an exemplary instance of what can be achieved by applying many of the approaches and techniques that were alluded to in the sections above:

> Two metrics stood out at the time – symbolising the desperate state the brand had reached: team turnover had reached 157% and less than one in three team members were fully trained and certified to their jobs! ... Frankly the previous management had been 'hiring hands not personalities and hearts and minds' trained and equipped to deliver *memorable guest experiences*... Today, team turnover hovers around 40%; team engagement is at an all-time high (we won the *Sunday Times*'s 'Top Big Company to Work For' Award in 2014); all of our restaurants achieved a 5-star 'Score on the Doors' environmental health rating in 2015 (an industry first within the casual dining sector!); we have opened 25 new restaurants and increased the EDITDA of the company from £4.2m to £30m (2015 calendar year) during the course of the turnaround! ...
>
> (Karen Forester, CEO, TGI Friday's, Case Study 18)

7.4 Stay Different – Maintain Experiential Distinctiveness

The effective brand leaders interviewed for this book all agreed that it was vital that strong brands delivered distinctive uplifting experiences that enabled them *be different* from their competitive set – but how did they advise meeting the challenge of *staying different*? After all, as Frank Steed pointed out in his powerful contributions concerning brand extinction in case studies 15 and 17, one the greatest danger for brands operating in similar segments and categories is that they eventually morph into a homogenous, undifferentiated mass; something that Ian Dunstall is increasingly finding in the UK today:

> A lot of brands get locked into what I call 'customer silos'; that is to say, their core customer grouping becomes their *only* customer set due to the mass migration of their secondary customers into more attractive segments of the market... This has happened a lot in UK hospitality, particularly in brands that once enjoyed broadly based appeal but have retrenched into servicing their core family market – a situation that has driven 'violent peaks' into a small number of dayparts, whilst leaving the rest of the time pretty slack (and hugely unprofitable)...
>
> (Ian Dunstall, brands guru, Case Study 11)

In addition, as was starkly illustrated in Chapter 5, brands can be driven into the abyss through gross mismanagement either (directly) through incompetent brand leaders (the so-called clueless, reckless, egoists or toxics) or 'vampire squid' type owners that starve the brand of financial resources due to their appetite for preposterous (and delusional) levels of return. So, returning to the question at the top, in addition to the qualifiers and differentiators we outlined for sustainability within the various chapters, what did our brand leaders stress as being the most important factors in ensuring strong food service brands stayed differentiated?

◘ *Retain your DNA* – the first thing that stands out is that, whilst advocating incremental change, our brand leaders urge that brands should *never* deviate from their 'true north' by diluting their 'core DNA'. What do they mean by this? Essentially, what they believe is that every brand has been founded *for a reason* in order to *address a core market* in a *distinctive manner.* Brand leaders should never lose sight of what the brand stands for and what it is seeking to do. Whilst they might innovate, they should do so without compromising the essence of the brand by, for instance, abandoning its core proposition and/or trashing its distinctive functional and emotional benefits (see above). Whilst brand leaders should subtly change the way in which they address the needs, feelings and aspirations of their staff and customers over time, they must also ensure that the brand stays true to its original 'heroic mission'. Abandoning its raison d'être will condemn the brand to the realms of ubiquity and irrelevance:

> The challenge is not to let the corporate governance interfere with the culture you have created from the beginning – the heart and soul of the business... Without that you have nothing!
>
> (Russel Joffe, founder, Giraffe, Case Study 6)

> It is my job to grow and stretch the brand whilst preserving its core DNA... ensuring it is consistently articulated throughout the business in whatever we do going forwards...
>
> (Tom Byng, founder and CEO, Byron, Case Study 9)

> Its owner has always been conscious to appoint somebody who has 'got its DNA' and will be its brand champion; warding off stupid short-termist, cost-engineering ideas that might take the brand back to the brink of oblivion...
>
> (Kevin Todd, ex-Director and General Manager, Toby Restaurants, Case Study 20)

> Brand essence understanding – ... Often brand leaders – desperate to halt the downwards spiral – have resorted to copying other brands... what they need to rediscover is where they came from and what their founding raison d'être was... Once this has been achieved, they can work on the nuances that will make it relevant in today's environment...
>
> (Philip Harrison, founder, Harrison Design, Case Study 21)

◘ *Be paranoid* - in conjunction with keeping an eye on staying true to its original mission, brand leaders all agreed that they had to constantly engender a feeling of restlessness and paranoia within both themselves and those around them to keep improving the brand. They saw complacency, incuriosity and laziness as their greatest enemies at every stage of the brand's lifecycle. Because, tellingly, the brand leaders interviewed for this book did not view continuous improvement as being only confined to the evolution stage of the brand: they believed that constant innovation within strong brands was a mantra that had to be applied from the get go:

> … we are not focussed on a breakneck speed of expansion; [but] rather, on continuing to be innovative…
>
> (Berry Casey, founder, Haché, Case Study 5)

> *Constant innovation* –… whilst we were scaling up the brand, we also kept listening to our customers and teams in the restaurants, and continued to keep fresh and exciting through constant innovation (menu development, 'proper' beer, monthly specials etc.)… this activity signalled to our new and existing customers that we were intent on keeping Byron interesting and relevant…
>
> (Tom Byng, founder and CEO, Byron, Case Study 9)

> Incremental change – I didn't go for any big-bang changes… instead, I focussed on a number of small incremental changes that would add up to quite a lot…
>
> (Andrew Emmerson, ex-MD, Millie's, Case Study 8)

> … we were always driven by a sense of healthy paranoia, a productive sense of fear about doing things better tomorrow…
>
> (Russel Joffe, founder, Giraffe, Case Study 6)

> Our view is that you cannot stand still in this market; people will always steal your ideas – you have to maintain a certain paranoia about continuing to innovate/do things differently to keep one step ahead!
>
> (Sue and Paul Salisbury, co-founders, Premium Country Dining Group, Case Study 10)

> … the one major attribute that DPG had was a fantastic culture that had been fostered by the CEO and his team – a healthy paranoia about keeping ahead of the competition… a hunger and real desire to anticipate or fix chinks in the armour that might prove costly in market-share terms in the long run…
>
> (Patricia Thomas, ex-Operations Director, Domino's Pizza, Case Study 13)

◘ *Flexibility from day one* - the whole point of brands is that should they form a 'bundle of recognisable attributes that somebody wants to buy' (Ambler and Styles 1996). To this extent – as our brand leaders stated above – a brand must present itself with a high level of coherence and consistency to consumers who seek an assured experience. Nevertheless, consumers are becoming more sophisticated and discriminating. They can value and appreciate difference not only between brands but *within* them as well. Thus, our brand leaders emphasised the need for some individuality between sites from day one – first, to increase levels of customer curiosity; and second, to give them design flexibility to stretch the brand into slightly different geographies and locations:

> ... the distinctiveness and quality of our offer allied to the fact that we have been prepared to customise our offer in various location (i.e. variable/seasonal pricing, different wine menus etc.) has kept up our forward momentum...
>
> (Andy Laurillard, founder, Giggling Squid, Case Study 5)

> Flexibility – another thing we have done from the get go is to recognise that we need to be flexible in terms of how and where we can fit the brand within particular locations. ... This means we must be flexible in our approach to scale and design; something that is highly important if we are going to rapidly expand.
>
> (Jamie Barber, founder, Cabana, Case Study 4)

> Concept flexibility – ... But we must always retain a degree of flexibility in two respects... First, when we open a new site, because 35% of our business is pre-booked, we find out pretty quickly customers' likes and dislikes... This enables us to go back in to reset a few things; which is fine because our concept runs on an 85% fixed, 15% flexible philosophy... Second, given the space constraints we are faced with, we have proof tested smaller formats which – while maintaining the essence of the brand – will enable us to access far more site opportunities going forwards...
>
> (Jillian McLean, founder, Drake & Morgan, Case Study 7)

◘ *Ambidexterity* - in their quest to stay different, especially when going through growth spurts or major 'makeover' events, brand leaders also highlighted the need for organisations to ensure that their core estate is decoupled from their development activities. This prevents distraction from delivering the numbers and protects any innovation from derailment. Also, as their organisations became larger, brand leaders saw it as their role to ensure that their brands were fit to discharge both efficiency *and* effectiveness. To this extent, brands should have a degree of 'ambidexterity' – in other words, the ability to simultaneously execute important activities that might seem completely antithetical.

> Efficiency AND creativity – perhaps one of the greatest challenges for evolving brands is the tension that will exist between the need for systematic efficiency juxtaposed against the requirement to stretch the concept through creative innovation in order to keep on trend... The Evolver must veer away from binary either/or solutions... S/he must insist that that brand members simultaneously attend to both vital processes without compromising either...
>
> (Vanessa Hall, CEO, YO! Sushi, Case Study 12)
>
> ....
>
> 'Skunk works' – one of the first decisions I took (stealing the idea from Apple at the time!) was to set up a completely separate entity outside of the brand... here we could think outside the box in a separate space and test out our ideas in a simulated environment (testing carving decks, ergonomic flows, new designs etc.)...
>
> (Kevin Todd, ex-Director and General Manager, Toby Restaurants,
> Case Study 20)

- ◘ *Blend your team* – finally, in a bid to stay different as the brand grew and evolved, brand leaders agreed that they needed to create a 'team of all the talents' (both newbie disrupters and long-timer experts) to drive their brand development forwards. Often the newbies might exhibit impatience with the slow pace of change and seem disrespectful to the ideals of the 'founding fathers'. Long timers, on the other hand, might be incredibly change averse and wedded to preserving and protecting irrational sacred cows. Brand leaders said that they needed both typologies to drive a composite approach to change, acknowledging that they would have to work hard to blend the team together to achieve optimal results:

Blended expert team – the turnaround team I assembled to populate this 'skunk works' included experienced internals (Ian Dunstall from Marketing; Sheelagh Pegg, Noel Darcey and Peter Leece from Operations; Karen Skingley from HR etc.) and expert externals (JRA, the interior design expert team; Deterministics, the throughput and capacity management experts; Roy Halstead Ass. Inc, the product development expert etc.)... They all offered different insights and perspectives. What we produced in the end was really an integrated team effort...

(Kevin Todd, ex-Director and General Manager, Toby Carvery, Case Study 20)

Generally, the CEO or MD of the brand will have assembled a team to tackle the brand reinvention challenge... Brand makeovers work best when leaders address every aspect of the business. In my experience, brands have usually lost touch and engagement with their guests at several levels: the service has drifted off, the product has become overly cost engineered and the environment lacks sparkle... The best way of solving this malaise is to take a multi-faceted, composite approach that addresses all aspects of the marketing mix to get it back on track...

(Philip Harrison, founder, Harrison Design, Case Study 21)

7.5 Final, Final Thoughts

We have set out our position on effective brand leadership in the main body of this book and then carefully triangulated the views of the brand leaders we interviewed during the course of our enquiry. So where does this finally leave us? If we were to identify the key ingredients for successful food service brand leaders throughout the lifecycle transitions of a brand, what would they be? Taking into account everything we've written and analysed in this book, we would highlight **four key characteristics of effective brand leaders**:

■ *They create distinctive uplifting experiences* – whatever the lifecycle stage of their brand, effective brand leaders understand that food service is, first and foremost, about creating *memorable customer experiences*. Possessing high levels of both IQ and EQ, they are able to address both the functional and emotional dimensions of their brand. From a functional point of view, they keep the brand *fresh* and relevant, constantly shaping and evolving their proposition (through menu and design innovation) without diluting its core positioning. From an emotional standpoint, they make working for the brand an *uplifting experience* for their staff who, in turn, create *uplifting experiences* for their guests. Hospitality is all about creating *happy, fulfilling and memorable shared experiences* for both staff and guests. Effective brand leaders get this! At the very least, the provision of out-of-home food service occasions, and the satisfaction they create, must exceed what customers could experience in their own homes – otherwise, what is their reason for existing?

- ◘ *They personify the brand* – another feature of effective brand leaders is the degree to which they *embody* and personify the brand. They authentically believe in what the brand stands for and what it is trying to achieve. They transmit *electricity* through the brand via their passion, pace and commitment; using powerful symbols, stories, heroes, myths and legends to connect emotionally with their team. Leading their brand isn't a job; it is a mission through which they intend – as Jens Hofma put it in Case Study 19 – to 'leave their mark'. Whether or not brand leaders are there at the start of the journey or have joined part-way through, their belief in their brand and its sustained success must be infectious and contagious!

- ◘ *They nurture leaders not followers* – through their actions and demeanour they create a cadre of leaders rather than followers. Food service involves multiple transactions, over multiple sites, involving multiple touch points. Things are unlikely to run smoothly from session to session even if units are set up correctly in terms of pre-opening quantity/quality of product and people. Effective brand leaders propagate a culture of *adjust and overcome* – meaning that whatever the obstacles in the way of providing happy, memorable customer experiences, staff know they must *take accountability for finding quick and effective solutions*!

- ◘ *They exploit deep tacit knowledge* – food service is an unusual sector in that it has a number of 'moving parts' that combine to create memorable customer experiences. Brand leaders must engineer sensory stimulants that, first, get customers to visit them rather than the competition and, second, make their out-of-home dining experience demonstrably better than staying in! But as Philip Harrison put it in Case Study 21, successful brands benefit from a 'composite, multi-faceted approach to their design and execution'. Brand leaders who want to be 'world class rather than Wolverhampton class' recruit the best: experts steeped in tacit (uncodified and generally unarticulated) knowledge who will take the brand to the next level. In addition, effective brand leaders will always respect the tacit knowledge of brand members who have been on the journey from the start. These people hold powerful insights into the brand's archaeology and 'how to get things done around here'!

In the end though, it comes down to this: brands are about people; both staff and customers. Great brands create great *symbiotic experiences* for both. As Jamie Barber reflected in Case Study 4, food service brands exist to 'lift people's spirits'! In an increasingly crowded food service marketplace, in order for brands to be different and stay different, effective brand leaders need – above all – to give people their **due**, namely: **d**istinctive **u**plifting **e**xperiences, whatever their brand's lifecycle positioning.

Bibliography

Ambler, T., and Styles, C. (1996) 'Brand development versus new product development: towards a process model of extension decisions'. *Marketing Intelligence and Planning*. 14(7), 10-19.

Bateson, J. (1985) 'Perceived Control and the Service Encounter' in Czepiel, J., Solomon, M., and Surprenant, C. (eds), *The Service Encounter: Managing Employee/Customer Interaction in Service Businesses*. Lexington MA: Lexington Books.

Berry, L. (2000) 'Cultivating Service Brand Equity'. *Academy of Marketing Science*. 28(1), 128-137.

Charity, P. (2015a) 'Chain Restaurant Numbers Increase by 258% in Seven Years'. Propel Info. 28 April.

Charity, P. (2015b) 'McDonald's Easterbrook Sets Out Turnaround Plan'. Propel Info. 4 May.

Charity, P. (2015c) 'Horizons – Now More Than 500 Emerging Food Service Brands in the UK'. Propel Info. 5 May.

Charity, P. (2015d) 'McDonald's Steve Easterbrook – There's More to Come on Turnaround Plan'. Propel Info. 7 May.

Charity, P. (2015e) 'CGA's Peach Market Growth Monitor – Reports Net New Openings of 1,770 Restaurants in Past 12 Months'. Propel Info. 22 September.

de Chernatony, L. (2001) 'A Model for Strategically Building Brands'. *Brand Management*. 9(1), 32–44.

de Chernatony, L., and McDonald, M. (1992) *Creating Powerful Brands*. London: Butterworth Heinemann.

de Chernatony, L., and Segal-Horn, S. (2003) 'The Criteria for Successful Services Brands'. *European Journal of Marketing*. 37(7/8), 1,095-118.

Edger, C. (2012) *Effective Multi-Unit Leadership – Local Leadership in Multi-Site Situations*. Farnham: Gower Business Publishing.

Edger, C. (2013) *International Multi-Unit Leadership – Developing Local Leaders in Multi-Site Operations*. Farnham: Gower Business Publishing.

Edger, C. (2014) *Professional Area Management – Leading at a Distance in Multi-Unit Enterprises* (1st Edition). Oxford: Libri.

Edger, C. (2015) *Professional Area Management – Leading at a Distance in Multi-Unit Enterprises* (2nd Revised Edition). Oxford: Libri.

Edger, C. (2016) *Area Management – Strategic and Local Models for Growth*. Oxford: Libri.

Edger, C., and Emmerson, A. (2015) *Franchising – How Both Sides Can Win*. Oxford: Libri.

Heskett, J., Jones, T., Loveman, G., Sasser, W., and Schlesinger, L. (1994) 'Putting the Service Profit Chain to Work'. *Harvard Business Review*. March–April, 164-74.

Johnson, G., and Scholes, K. (1993) *Exploring Corporate Strategy*. London: Prentice Hall.

Jones, P. (1999) 'Multi-unit management in the hospitality industry: a late twentieth century phenomenon'. *International Journal of Contemporary Hospitality Management*. 11(4), 155-64.

Jones, P., Hillier, D., Shears, P., and Clarke-Hill, C. (2002) 'Customer Perceptions of Services Brands: A Case Study of the Three Major Fast Food Retailers in the UK'. *Management Research News*. 25(6/7), 41-9.

Kotter, J. (1996) *Leading Change*. Harvard Business Review Press.

Kroc, R. (1997/1977) *Grinding It Out*. Chicago: St Martin's.

Lechner, C., and Kreutzer, M. (2010) Coordinating Growth Initiatives in Multi-Unit Firms. *Long Range Planning*. 43, 6-32.

Levitt, T. (1980) 'Marketing Success through Differentiation – of Anything'. *Harvard Business Review*. January–February.

Lincoln, G., and Elwood, C. (1995) 'Branding Pubs – Can it Work?' *International Journal of Wine Marketing*. 7(2), 5-20.

McKinsey (2006) 'The "Moment of Truth" in Customer Service'. *McKinsey Quarterly*. February.

McKinsey (2008) 'Maintaining the Customer Experience'. *McKinsey Quarterly*. December.

Meyer, D. (2010) *Setting the Table: The Transforming Power of Hospitality in Business*. New York: Harper.

Muller, C. (1998) 'Endorsed Branding: The Next Step in Restaurant-Brand Management'. *Cornell Hotel and Restaurant Quarterly*. 39(3), 90-6.

Muller, C. (2013) *The Leader of Managers – Leading in a Multi-Unit, Multi-Site and Multi-Concept World*. Boston: HAP.

O'Reilly, C., and Tushman, M. (2004) 'The Ambidextrous Organisation'. *Harvard Business Review*. April, 74-81.

Pink, D. (2011) *The Surprising Truth About What Motivates Us*. Edinburgh: Canongate.

Reichheld, F. (2003) 'The One Number You Need to Grow'. *Harvard Business Review*. December.

Reynolds, J., Howard, E., Cuthbertson, C., and Hristov, L. (2007) 'Perspectives on Retail Format Innovation: Relating Theory and Practice'. *International Journal of Retail and Distribution Management*. 35(8), 647-60.

Sasser, W., Olsen, R., and Wyckoff, D. (1978) *Management of Service Operations: Text, cases and readings*. Boston MA: Allyn and Bacon.

Schultz, H. (2008/1998) *Pour Your Heart into It: How Starbucks Built a Company One Cup at Time*. New York: Hyperion.

Sharp, B. (2010) *How Brands Grow: What Marketers Don't Know*. Melbourne: OUP.

Steiner, R. (2011) 'Room at the Top in Corporate UK'. *Daily Mail*. 23 November, 73.

Wilkinson, M. (2013) *The Ten Principles Behind Great Customer Experiences*. Harlow: FT Publishing.

Index